Why? Wait! ...on true love?

by Josh McDowell with Dr. Ralph Woodworth

In easy-to-read International English,
a 1,500 word vocabulary of basic English words.

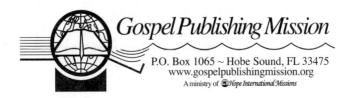

Gospel Publishing Mission

P.O. Box 1065 ~ Hobe Sound, FL 33475
www.gospelpublishingmission.org
A ministry of Hope International Missions

For information about other International English books
visit our web site at:
www.gospelpublishingmission.org

Unless otherwise indicated, Scripture references are from the Holy Bible,
New Life Version, Copyright © 1969, 1976, 1983, 1986, 1992, 1997,
Christian Literature International. P.O. Box 777, Canby, OR 97013.
Used by permission.

Derived from: *Why True Love Waits,* by Josh McDowell
Copyright 1987, 2002 by Josh McDowell.

Josh McDowell Ministry, P.O. Box 131000, Dallas, TX 75313
www.josh.org
Original publishers: Here's Life Publishers, Inc. 1987, Tyndale House
Publishers, Inc. 2002

Joseph E. Taylor, *Editor-in-chief*
Ralph L. Woodworth, Ph.D, *Editor/Translator*

COVER ART BY ROBERT SCOTT / CLEAR GRAPHICS
(859) 363-3955

Why Wait? ...on true love?
IN INTERNATIONAL ENGLISH

ISBN: 978-1-933716-11-4

Contents

Chapter 1
Why Does True Love Wait?

Everyone likes Derek, especially the girls. Derek had many girlfriends before he met Michelle. Now she is his only one. They seem to be together all the time. The unusual thing about Derek is that he is 20 years old and still a virgin. That is, he has never had sex. As a Christian, he knows that sex before marriage is wrong. Michelle is a Christian also, and Derek is sure he will marry her some day.

Not long ago Derek was witnessing to his friend Colin. Colin asked, "If I become a Christian will I have to stop having sex with my girlfriend?" They talked about that for a long time. Colin explained that he and his girlfriend both felt that having sex added so much to their relationship. She was taking birth-control medicine, so there was no danger of getting pregnant.

Colin's question troubled Derek. He began to ask himself why he and Michelle should wait for marriage. He wondered if the Bible's teaching about sex was just for those days long ago. Perhaps those teachings were not meant for us in our day, he thought.

Derek finally decided that God knows all about us and has our best interests at heart. "I decided that I just had to wait for God even if I did not understand His reasons," he said.

Annie is another Christian who is still a virgin. Although she is 17 years old and very pretty, she has never had many dates. She knows God has called her to be a missionary, and she will not date a boy who is not a serious Christian. She has always been willing to wait for the man God would choose for her. Several months ago Jeff, a nice-looking young soldier, started coming into the shop where Annie works after school. Several times he had asked her for a date, but she had always refused.

Annie had witnessed to Jeff several times but was still surprised when he told her one day that he had accepted Christ. After that he started attending Annie's church. It seemed that he could not get enough of church and Bible study. When he asked her again for a date, she felt that she could not refuse. In fact, she did not want to refuse. Jeff was becoming the kind of man she had been asking God to send to her.

Soon Annie knew that she was deeply in love with the young soldier. Then Jeff started asking her to show her love by having sex. She knew it was wrong, but she did not know how to explain that to him. She went to her pastor's wife for help. "I have never questioned God's directions about sex until now," Annie said. "I have never really been tempted before. But now – well, Jeff is so different from the other boys I have known. Why does God say to wait until marriage when you are as deeply in love as Jeff and I are?"

Like Derek and Annie, many Christian young people wonder why God says to wait until marriage to have sex. All their friends seem to be sexually active. That is true even of their Christian friends. Society seems to expect unmarried young people to be sexually active. It even urges them to be.

After all, people argue, the Bible is a very old book. Many things have changed since the Bible was written, they say. We no longer need to follow the teachings of the Bible in every point, they say. Sex is just a way of showing love.

Those are the two main problems for Christian young people: the age of the Bible and the meaning of true love.

The Bible is a very old book, but it is no older than the problem of sexual sin. The reasons for the rules God gave in the Bible still fit the conditions of today. God did not give those rules about sex because of the way people lived in those days or the kind of work they did. He gave those rules because men are men and women are women. God made men to be drawn toward women and women toward men. That has not changed.

What we need to understand is why God gave the rules about sex. God loves us. Because He loves us, He wants to protect us from the bad things that happen if we use sex in the wrong way. That wrong use of sex can lead to guilt, pain and unwanted babies. It can lead to disease and even death.

God also wanted to provide for us the very best use and enjoyment of sex. He knows that the most enjoyable sex is between one man and one woman in a faithful marriage relationship. He never gives rules in order to keep us from having fun. God's way is a satisfying, happy way!

Most Christian young people accept some limits on sexual activity. They agree that having sex with a number of different people is clearly wrong. They agree that unmarried people should not have babies together or have abortions. They agree that we should not take a chance of getting a serious disease through the wrong use of sex.

The question for them is, why is it wrong for two people who are deeply in love to show that love by having sex? Does true love make sex right? I shock many parents when I say that I agree that true love does make sex right. The problem is that most young people do not have a right understanding of true love.

What is God's understanding of true love? The Bible tells what true love does and what it does not do:

Love does not give up. Love is kind. Love is not jealous. Love does not put itself up as being important. Love has no pride. Love does not do the wrong thing. Love never thinks of itself. Love does not get angry. Love does not remember the suffering that comes from being hurt by someone. Love is not happy with sin. Love is happy with the truth (1 Corinthians 13:4-6).

Other Scriptures such as Romans 13:10, Matthew 7:12 and Philippians 2:4 also show what the Bible means by true love. True love is making the happiness and good of another person as important as our own. True love is to love others as God loves us. Anyone who uses love as an excuse for sex outside of marriage is not speaking of true love at all.

Troubling Facts

More than one in ten young people in the United States have had sex before they reach the age of 14. By the time they reach age 18, more than six in ten have had sex at least once. For nearly two out of ten of those, they had sex for the first time with someone they did not know or had just met. Half of them have had sex with more than one person.[1] Many young people are sexually active for about eight years before they get married.[2]

Between 1971 and 1988, the women between the ages of 15 and 19 who had had sex at least once increased by 66 percent.[3] More than three out of four pregnancies among women between those ages happened outside of marriage. Three out of ten of those pregnancies ended in abortion.[4]

There Is Good News

In 1995 a study found that 50 percent of women between the ages of 15 and 19 had had sexual intercourse.[5] That was down from 53 percent in 1988. The number of unmarried men who had had sex fell from 60 percent to 55 percent in the same period.[6] That is not much lower, but it is lower. It was the first time in many years that the rate had fallen.

Another study found that 44 percent of young people had decided to delay sex.[7] As a result there were fewer pregnancies among young people and fewer abortions. Young people are learning that it is possible to control sexual desires.[8]

A recent study found that almost half of the young people questioned said that sex before marriage is always wrong.[9] More and more young people are saying that being a virgin is a good thing.[10] These findings show that young people are beginning to reject the free-love ideas that have been so common in the recent past.

Why Are Young People Deciding to Delay Sex?

A group of 18- and 19-year-old men and women were asked why they had decided to delay having sex. They gave many reasons. Half of them said they were afraid of having a baby. Two out of ten said they were waiting until marriage for religious reasons. Two out of ten said that it was too early in their relationship to have sex. Nearly four out of ten, mostly men, said that their boyfriend or girlfriend was not willing to have sex.[11]

The ones who felt the best about still being virgins were those who waited for religious reasons. They admitted that they had normal sexual desires but were determined to control those desires.

Many other reasons are given to explain why young people are delaying sex. One of the greatest is the fear of getting a serious disease. There is good reason for that fear. While sex among young people is happening less often, sexually transmitted diseases (STDs) are on the increase.[12]

Broken Hearts, Shattered Hopes

I get letters from many young people who have not waited. Here are just a few of them.

Sex gave me fear as a gift and shame to wear as a covering. It robbed me of peace of mind and took away my hope of a bright future. It destroyed my ability to listen in class. It took away any interest in church. It cheated me of my faith in Christ. It crushed my trust in people. Sex gave me a terrible wound in my heart that even now seven years later, has never healed.

* * * * *

Can you help me? I am 13 and I have just ruined my life. I thought Mike really loved me. He said he did. Last night we had sex for the first time, and this morning he told my friend that he did not want to see me any more. I thought giving him what he wanted would make him love me more. What if I am pregnant? I cannot talk to my parents. What is going to happen to me? I feel so alone and I do not know what to do.

* * * * *

Pregnancy outside of marriage is frightening and lonely.

* * * * *

I had sex for the first time at a very young age. In doing so I ruined another person's marriage and family life. Now I have an STD that I will have for the rest of my life and probably will never be able to have children. I live with feelings of guilt. Finally I have learned how harmful sex outside of marriage can really be.

* * * * *

I love him. He said that he loved me too. But after we had sex, he called me all kinds of bad names and left me. I do not understand. We went together for months before we had sex. I thought we had something special. Now I have this feeling that no one cares about me and that I will never be able to make any man happy.

* * * * *

This girl told her story as if she were talking about another person.

She was very young, but she did not feel young. When she turned 13, she felt so grown up and she loved it. She was near the top of her class at school and always took part in all the after-school activities. Her parents were good people and had taught her right from wrong. Everyone thought she was a good girl who would never get into any kind of trouble.

He was older and very popular. He could do anything, and in any group he was the one people always watched. He could have any girl in the school. When he started taking a special interest in her, she could not believe it. One day he said, "I love you." But she did not love him. She only liked having people watch her because she was with him.

He asked if he could express his love for her. She said she was not ready. Later he told her he had shown his love to another girl. She did not object. Again he said, "I love you." She believed him, but she said nothing.

She enjoyed being his girlfriend. So many people wanted to talk with her because she was with him. She had never had so many friends before. Other boys started talking to her, too, but she was loyal to him because he loved her.

15

Again he told her that he had shown his love to another girl. But he did not really love that girl, he said. "I love only you." This time she looked at the ground and said softly, "I love you, too." He said, "Then show your love." She did not want to do it, but she was afraid she would lose him to another girl. So she showed her love.

After it was over she felt dirty. She was no longer innocent. She stopped dating him. He begged her to take him back. He said, "I love you." But she refused him. A few days later he was in love with another girl. She felt so ashamed for what she had done. She was covered all over by guilt. She was very much alone.

She knows she can never change the past. She has damaged her life, and it can never be repaired.

She was very young. Finally she understood how very young she was.

* * * * *

Here is a letter that gives the picture from the boy's side.

If only I had waited. I see now how my life would have been so much better. I see how my mind would have been free from this memory that troubles me even years later.

If you want to know what it is really like, glue two pieces of paper together. After the glue has dried, pull the papers apart. That is a picture of two people after having sex. They are both torn, leaving part of themselves with the other.

Two things were always the same every time I had a different girlfriend. We had sex often, and every time we ended our friendship I went through terrible pain. That pain is still with me.

The first time it happened I was 17. I thought I was so great because this girl had agreed to have sex with me. Then she started talking about how much she loved me. She started holding on to me as though she were never going to let me go. That is when I started to think that I was probably not the first for her. There were probably other boys before me, maybe many others. She was probably just using me to satisfy her own need for security.

I could not think very highly of anyone who gave in as easily as she had. After four weeks of having sex with her as often as I wanted, I was tired of her. I left her, but that made me feel even worse because I could see that she was hurting. I knew that her home life was not very good. Probably she found no satisfaction or security there.

Over the following months I had many different girls. But I never thought about the girl I would marry someday or what I would tell her. I never thought that she might care about being the first girl I had ever been with.

This man could have saved himself and his future wife a lifetime of pain if someone had given him a good reason to wait.

A young man talked with me after hearing me speak. "What you said really made me see some things," he said. "If I could have just one wish, it would be to be 12 years old again and hear this same talk. I have made some bad choices, and now I am feeling the pain from those choices."

Looking for Reasons to Wait

Most of the young people I hear who say they are not sure about sex are Christians like Derek and Annie. They attend church, read their Bibles and pray. They share their faith. They know that sex before marriage is wrong, but they do not know why it is wrong. Here are some of their stories.

I had been told all my life that sex before marriage was wrong, but no one ever told me why it was wrong. When I was in my last year of high school, I started dating one boy. As we spent time alone together, we started to have sex. I felt guilty, bitter and dirty. I would say to him, "We need to stop having sex, or at least slow down." We tried to slow down, but that did not work.

After two years I finally said, "No more sex." He said, "Goodbye." After that, whenever I dated another man for any length of time, we always had sex. Each time I had sex I would cry later because I knew that I had failed again.

* * * * *

I was almost 18 and was still a virgin. I had just never wanted to have sex. Then I fell in love with a nice-looking man several years older than me. He would sometimes say that he had never dated a girl who said no as many times as I had. Finally I weakened since I could not give any good reason not to do so. Saying "yes" was easier than trying to explain why I was saying "no."

Young people need to know more than just the difference between right and wrong. They need to know why right is right and wrong is wrong. They need to know why sex before marriage is wrong. What is more, they want to know. One study asked the students in the school system of Atlanta, Georgia, what they most wanted in a sex-education program. Most of them answered that they wanted to know "how to say no to sex before marriage."

What has been happening to young people in general has been happening to church young people as well. Most young people who grow up in the church do not understand why the Bible says they should wait until marriage for sex. When they are tempted to have sex, they cannot understand why they should not.

They do not understand the Bible's teaching about sex. They do not understand how sex before marriage can damage their emotional life. They do not understand how sex before marriage can lead to many health problems. They only know that their friends are doing it and they do not want to be different.

In this book we will help young people count the cost of sex before marriage. We will explore the many reasons why young people become sexually active. We will then explain why true love waits for sex until marriage. Finally, we will discuss ways for young people to say no to sex before marriage.

Chapter 2
Young People and Sex Before Marriage

What if a boy came to his father to tell of a very dangerous game he and his friends were playing? The game might end in death. In fact, the boy says that one of his friends has already died playing the game. What would you think if the father just warned his son to "be careful"? The danger is too great for a simple warning to be careful. A good father would do his best to keep his son from playing such a dangerous game.

Yet young people who have sex before marriage are playing just such a game. It may seem like fun to them. It may be exciting. Maybe they will not die from it, but they will get hurt in some very serious ways.

Young people who have sex before marriage will pay a price. That is guaranteed. The cost in guilt, pain, unhappiness and possible disease or death is too high. But the young people face real temptation and get great pressure from other young people. That makes them forget what their sin will cost them. That is why we must answer their questions about sex. We must help them understand God's reasons for waiting for sex until they are married.

One very big problem with sex before marriage is that when that person gets married, usually the marriage will not last very long. Young people who wait for sex have a better chance of enjoying a lasting, satisfying marriage than those who do not wait.

In the rest of this chapter, we will study two of the highest costs of sex before marriage. They are the possibility of disease and the possibility of pregnancy. These are two of the biggest problems in our world today. As a result, sex outside of marriage has become a leading health problem.

Many young people know that sex before marriage can cause diseases and unwanted pregnancies. But that does not stop most of them. They simply are not concerned. Nor does their concern increase with age or with the amount of sexual activity they have. They pay a high price, though, long after the fun has gone.

The Cost of Diseases and Possible Death

A young married man who is not a Christian came to see me. He told me to keep telling people what I was telling them about sex. When I asked him why, he told me his sad story:

> When I was young I was careless about how I lived. I had sex with many women. Then I heard about herpes, a disease that comes through having sex. I knew I could never get rid of it if I got it. But I did not change my way of living.
>
> Then I learned that there was a new kind of herpes. You could have it without even knowing it unless you had a baby. Then the baby might be born with serious health problems. Even then I did not change my way of living.
>
> Then AIDS came. It can kill you! That really made me think. Finally I decided to stop having sex with so many women. I decided to find one woman I really liked, get married and have children. That is what I did. Then my wife gave me herpes.

The Rapid Spreading of Sex-Caused Diseases

One of the most harmful and permanent results of sex before marriage is getting an STD. There are as many as thirty STDs that are passed from one person to another through sex. More than 15 million people in America get an STD each year. One in four of those people are under 20 years of age. Sixty-eight million Americans now have one of the diseases.[1] Fifty-eight million of those have an STD that cannot be cured through medicine.[2]

One student wrote to me:

> If you have sex with many different people, you open yourself up to many kinds of diseases. That is also true if you have sex with just one person if that person has had sex with many different people. Those diseases may seem like only a small problem. But they may be hard or impossible to get rid of. Or they may kill you. But if you sleep around long enough, you will probably get something.

Let us look especially at how these STDs are affecting our young people. About half of our young people are having sex, and about one-fourth to one-third of these have an STD. As those who have an STD have sex with those who do not, that number is growing. Young people are only about 10 percent of the American population, but they have 25 percent of the cases of STDs. Sixty percent of Americans who have HIV caught it before they were 20 years old.

Studies show that the younger a person is when he starts having sex, the more different people he will have sex with over time. But having sex with many people greatly increases the possibility of getting an STD. That makes the cost of having sex before marriage too high. We must show our young people how true love can wait.

Young Women Are in Greater Danger

Linda, 19, was unmarried. She went to the doctor because of the great pain in the lower part of her body. The doctor found a large growth inside her body that was caused by an STD. He operated on her to remove the growth and repair the parts of her body that had been damaged. He warned her that she probably would never be able to have children. She had always dreamed of having children but had to give up that dream. That was a high price to pay for her sexual experiences with many men.[3]

That story touches me deeply because I have three daughters. Think about the young girls in your family, your church or your classroom. Many of them are sweet, innocent and full of life. Like Linda, the exciting, life-filling experiences of school, marriage and mothering are yet before them. But these young women may have to pay an especially high price for sex before marriage.

Girls are not as sexually active as boys are. But because of the way their bodies are made, girls are more in danger of getting STDs than boys are. We must protect these girls and young women by helping them see the importance of waiting for sex until marriage.

Here are some important facts about young women and sexual disease:

- Women get sexual diseases more than men do because their bodies are slower to show signs of the disease.[4] That makes them delay getting medical treatment.

- The rates of cancer that may come from an STD are increasing among young women.[5]

- One study reported that 38 percent of sexually active women between 13 and 21 years of age already had an incurable sexual disease that is connected to certain cancers.[6]

- Women who get a sexual disease while pregnant may have their baby before it is fully developed. That can cause other health problems. It is believed that 30 percent to 40 percent of very early births and the deaths of babies at birth are caused by sexual disease.[7]

For the good of our daughters and other young women, we must help all young people say no to sexual pressure and sex before marriage.

Blind to How Terrible STDs Are

Many of our young people do not seem to understand the terrible cost of their sexual activity. This is especially true of our young women. With "safe sex" being taught in the public schools today, it would seem that Americans would be especially well educated about sexual diseases. That is not true.

In 1993 a national study asked 1,000 women from 18 through 60 years of age what they knew about STDs.[8] Almost two-thirds knew nothing or very little about sexual diseases other than HIV/ AIDS. Only 11 percent knew that sexual diseases can be more harmful to women than to men.

In another study only 11 percent of young people said that their parents had told them about STDs.[9] Yet 70 percent of students in their last year of high school were sexually active, and 27 percent had had sex with four or more people.

One report says, "Many teachers carried a 1960s and 1970s belief with them in developing sex education. They said that 'each person is free to make his own decisions.' They added that we should not judge people for their sexual actions. Young people, they said, should decide for themselves about sexual activities based on their own ideas of right or wrong."[10]

As a result, most sexually active Americans have decided that there is not much danger in being sexually active.[11] For example, 72 percent of young women between the ages of 18 and 24 were not concerned about getting an STD.

It is clear that our young people are not getting the facts they need to know about being sexually active. They must get those facts

24

and guidance from their homes, youth groups and churches. We must get the word to them before they are harmed by becoming sexually active.

Other Dangerous Ways to Have Sex

Many young people think they can have sex in safe ways. But it is possible to get an STD without going all the way in the sex act.

Thirteen-year-old Amy told her mother she had never had sex with her boyfriend. Then she began to have health problems. When her mother took her to the doctor, he said that she would have to have surgery. She had damage from an STD. Amy had to have two surgeries before the problem was corrected. Even so she would continue to suffer for the rest of her life.

Amy still said that she had never had sex with her boyfriend. They had just played around, she said, touching each other's private parts with their hands and mouths.

What students like Amy do not understand is that sexual diseases can be spread from one person to another without completing the sex act. The germs that cause the diseases are in the fluids that come from the body in the sex act.[12] Those germs can enter another body through a small cut, even the smallest opening in the skin.[13]

Young people need to be taught how dangerous such playing around is. If they do not understand the cost, they will continue to put themselves in harm's way.

The Cost of an Unwanted Baby

Tina and Wade planned to get married after they finished school. She was a Christian and had never had sex. She thought getting pregnant would be the worst thing that could ever happen to her. She was sorry for several girls she knew who had gotten pregnant. But she knew they had been having sex for several years. It was not surprising that they finally got pregnant and left school. Now they were very unhappy. She did not want to follow their example.

When the school year was almost over, Wade took Tina to a little house he had borrowed for the night. He built a fire and made things very nice. Then he surprised Tina with a costly ring. He said it was to show her that he really planned to marry her. She was so happy and filled with love that she began to cry. Wade asked her if they could have sex just once. She began to weaken. *Just one time,* she thought, *what could it hurt?* She also wanted to thank Wade for his kindness. So she gave in.

Two months later Tina confessed to her mother that she was pregnant. She told the whole story. "I did not think it would happen," she cried. "I do not sleep around, Mother. I only did it once. It is not fair!"

The Sad News about Young People's Pregnancies

Getting pregnant before marriage is one of the biggest problems sexually active young people have. Here are some of the letters I have received:

> The terrible truth among pregnant girls at my school is that many thought they would not get pregnant if they had sex only once. Some of them felt that only "bad girls" got pregnant.

* * * * *

> When I left my baby at the hospital the day after he was born, I left part of me with him.

26

I learned the hard way. Abortion deals with the situation at the time. But it never ends the guilt. It never breaks the tie between a mother and her baby.

It is true that the number of pregnancies among young women has gone down. But we must receive this good news with care. The problem now is that young girls who become pregnant are less likely to be married than in years past. Saying that young girls' pregnancies and births have gone down is like a country at war saying the death rate in battle is going down. It may seem like good news at first, but soldiers are still dying in the fighting. The war is not over.

In the same way, unmarried young women continue to get pregnant at a high rate. With every unwanted pregnancy there are at least three problems: the girl, the boy and the child they have created. They will have to deal not only with the pregnancy but with many emotional and family problems as well. If Tina allows her child to be born, that baby's life will be affected by the conditions of his creation. As long as girls like Tina are getting pregnant, the war is not over. So we must continue to urge our young people to wait for sex until they are married.

The Hard Road of Young Girls as Mothers

If Tina decides to give birth to the child, she will be like many other young women in our country. One writer said, "In 1960, one out of twenty American children was born outside of marriage. Today it is almost one out of three. If we fail to act, in ten years it will be one of two."[14]

The rate of babies born to young girls in the United States is the highest of that in any industrial nation.[15] It is nearly two times as great as that of England and fifteen times that of Japan.

27

Today, over 75 percent of the births to women through the age of 19 are to unmarried women.[16]

Young people like Tina and Wade are not prepared to have children. The pressures of being parents at such a young age are just too great. We will examine some of those pressures in the next chapter. In chapter 11 we will discuss in full the sadness of young girls as mothers.

The Dead-end Road of Abortion

Tina has another very costly way to deal with her pregnancy. Like millions of young women before her, Tina can choose to abort her unborn child. There are many people who will try very hard to help her do that. In much of our country a 16-year-old girl cannot receive pain medicine from the school nurse without her parents' approval. Yet the same girl can receive an excuse from school to have an abortion without her parents knowing about it.

But abortion comes at a huge price to the young woman. I am not talking about the doctor's fee. During the killing of their unborn children, women have died on the abortion table. For those who live through it, there are many possible health problems. Many women are not able to have children later. Then there are the guilt and sorrow of murdering one's own child. Consider the sad situation of a young woman whose story was sent to me:

> I had an abortion when I was 16. Later, when I got married, I wanted very much to have my own family. After a time of trying to get pregnant and not being able to do so, I went to a doctor. What he discovered left me so unhappy. The abortion must have caused tissue from the surgery to build up and close the way that leads to my uterus. My body had defended itself with that tissue so that there would be no future abortion or pregnancy. The doctor had no other way to explain my problem.

What a terrible price to pay for a few minutes of sexual fun.

The cost of sex before marriage to our young people is almost too great to be counted. They are playing with their health, their future and their very lives. We must do whatever we can to help them stop this. But others also are paying when our children are doing wrong. In the next chapter we will examine the high price to us – the families, churches, schools and towns involved with these young people.

Chapter 3
The High Cost of Sex Before Marriage

A young person's life can be hurt by just a few hours of sexual enjoyment. Let us think about how Tina's life changed by what she did with Wade. Tina is not a real person, but she is like many young people who have talked with me.

Ten years after Tina and Wade spent the night in that little house she is 27 years old. With the help of her parents, she decided two very important things during the first three months of her pregnancy. First, she decided not to abort the baby. As a Christian, she felt terrible about having sex before marriage and getting pregnant. She was not about to add murder through abortion.

The second thing she decided was to separate from Wade. He had tried to get her to have an abortion. When she would not agree, he got angry. He told her, "If you really love me, you will do what I want. We can have children later, but I do not want to be responsible for them now." That made Tina think differently about him. So she gave back the ring he had given her. They never spoke to each other again. Tina has had only a few dates with men since then.

The first three years after Kristin was born, Tina lived with her parents. Then she got a job and she and Kristin moved into a small house she rented. One time she lost her job and had to have help from the government. She felt bad about that, but now she is working again and hopes for better times. She never had time to finish high school.

If her parents did not give her money now and then, her situation would be worse. They have invited her to come back and live with them again. But she would like to remain independent if possible, though she is weakening. She understands how it would save money. She also sees how it would be good for Kristin to be with her grandmother and grandfather. She thinks she might move back home at the end of the month.

Even though her situation is difficult, Tina knows she has much to be thankful for. For one thing, she is happy she does not have an STD. Another thing is that she loves Kristin very much and feels it was right to give birth to her and raise her. She is thankful she did not continue to be sexually active and get pregnant again. Her situation would have been even worse.

The High Costs to a Young Unmarried Mother

There is a 70 percent chance that the unmarried young mother will never finish high school. Think of how that will affect her chances of ever getting a good job.[1] The possibility for marriage goes down, too, because a man would have to take not only a wife but a child as well.

An unmarried young mother will probably need help from the government. One report says that 77 percent of unmarried young mothers will receive government help within five years of giving birth.[2] The possibility is even greater for younger girls. Money problems are only half the story. Think of the emotional cost of being so poor.

One study says there is a 25 percent chance that an unmarried young mother will have a second child within two years. That will only add to her problems.

It is almost a sure thing that the unmarried young mother will end up living with her parents, grandparents or other older people.[3] These girls need the money and emotional help of older people for months or years to come. Think of the cost to parents to have to care for both their child and their grandchildren.

A price has to be paid for sinning. A young person's mind and emotions are affected when he or she takes part in sexual actions. The mind does not forget. There is also guilt for what has been done to the other person. God's rules and commands have been violated. That really hurts young people who are Christians. They cannot witness and have God's blessing until they are right with God again. We must do our part to protect girls like Tina from the terrible costs of sex before marriage.

The High Cost to the Child

Let us take a closer look at Kristin, the child born to Tina and Wade before marriage. What price will she pay for her parents' sin? For one thing, she may never know her father. Tina has told her a little about Wade. Kristin sometimes says she hopes to meet him some day. If Tina gets angry with Kristin, Kristin says she will run away and live with her father when she knows where he is. Tina does not believe her, but her words still hurt.

Kristin does not do well in school. She also has been in trouble for hitting other students who call her names. The school says this is common in one-parent homes.

Tina is concerned about Kristin's friends, too. Tina has tried to control the situation. This causes trouble between her and Kristin. So Tina lets her go, knowing that her friends fill the empty time after school before Tina gets home from work. Tina does not know that Kristin's best friend also comes from a one-parent home. The friend has been teaching Kristin about sex, drugs and other bad things.

It is a sad situation. Kristin is sharing the cost of her parents' sex before marriage. A number of studies give a more complete picture of the possible problems these innocent children face. Here are some of the biggest problems:

If one of the parents has an STD, the baby may be born blind. Or it may be born with the STD one of the parents has. Some children of unmarried mothers come into the world already needing drugs or alcohol. These children are in trouble even before they are born.

Pregnant young women do not take care of themselves as well as older mothers do. This can lead to low birth weight or even death. It can cause serious problems with the health and well-being of the child. These children are two times more likely to be treated badly than those born to mothers over 20.[4] They are two to three times more likely to run away from home before they are old enough to provide for themselves. Many have to be provided for by others. Such children cost the government as much as $900 million a year.[5]

One study shows that girls born to young mothers are 83 percent more likely to become young mothers themselves than those born to women older than 20.[6] If they do not become mothers while they are young, they still are 50 percent more likely to have children before marriage.[7]

In our world, so many unborn children pay the greatest price for their parents' sexual sin: death through abortion. In the United States alone the lives of more than a million unborn babies are ended every year through abortion.

God must be very sad to see these innocent children, born and unborn, paying such a price for their parents' sin. But when we do not follow God's loving commands, someone always has to pay the price.

The High Cost to Others

American taxpayers are paying a high price for young people's sex before marriage. Each year in America about $17 billion is spent on all STDs and their results. That comes to about $240 a year for a family of four. That does not include other costs like time lost from work. The price is too high when it is for a problem that could be prevented easily.

In 1998 taxpayers were spending $2,831 a year for each young unmarried mother.[8] This is not free sex. It is costly sex. You and I are paying for it. Most of these costs would be unnecessary if young people waited until marriage for sex.

According to many people, sex is a private act between two people. They say that no one has the right to tell other people how they should act. We are told that the government has no right to make laws that affect a person's private sexual actions. We are told that schools should not be allowed to teach that young people should not have sex before marriage.

Sex at public cost is not a private act. It is not private when people who have sex behind closed doors demand that the government spend billions of dollars on finding a cure for AIDS. It is no longer private when girls become pregnant behind closed doors and pass the costs of their children on to taxpayers.

Even worse, sex is no longer private when one or both partners get an STD and then pass it to other people in other "private acts." Many times young people do not know they are carrying an STD. That is why young people need to know the complete sexual history of the other person before they marry.

A businessman came to me one day. He said he had been having sex with several women. When his wife found out, she was deeply hurt and angry. To get back at him, she had sex with their neighbor. That man gave her an STD. Then she passed the disease on to her husband. He was deeply hurt and knew that he was paying a high price for his sin. God said long ago, "He who does sex sins with a woman does not think well. He who does it is destroying himself"(Proverbs 6:32).

34

Only in a marriage can sex between two persons even come close to being considered a private act.

After a meeting with a group of high school students in Orlando, Florida, a big, nice-looking young man came to me. I will call him Jed. He was crying as he told me that his whole life he had tried to get his father to put his arms around him and tell him, "I love you." He never did. So, about six months ago Jed joined the army.

He got so lonely in the army that when he met this girl, he had sex with her. She gave him an STD. Then he really cried. He said that that was the only time in his life he had ever done something like that. He told me he was a Christian. He asked if anyone will ever love him.

I really felt sorry for this young man. He will have to deal with his disease for the rest of his life. He may end up living an unmarried life for fear he might hurt a wife. He will miss out on the joys of being a husband, father and grandfather. His one minute of weakness will be very costly to him.

It may be too late for Jed, although God has forgiven him and can still use him. It is not too late for many of our young people if they will wait for sex until marriage.

Chapter 4
Children in Grown-up Bodies

Fourteen-year-old Craig was pleased with the changes that were taking place in his body. Just a year ago he looked like a boy. Now he was beginning to look like a man. He was beginning to feel like a man, too, especially when he was around girls.

His feelings about girls were changing also. He no longer wanted to stay away from girls or make trouble for them when he was near them. Now he liked to be near girls. He liked to look at them and talk with them. He especially liked to look at Drew, the new girl in one of his classes at school. He thought about her often and wondered what it would be like to be with her.

Drew, too, was pleased and excited about the changes taking place in her body. She saw that boys, mostly the older boys and even some men, watched her. That pleased her. She laughed, though, at the look on their faces when they learned that she was only 14. She was especially pleased when she saw Craig watching her. She tried not to let him know that she might be interested in him.

Craig and Drew are too young to be allowed to drive a car. They are too young to vote or buy tobacco or alcohol. In many ways they are still children, but they are living in adult bodies. Their bodies are able to have sex and even to have children. Many young people their age are doing just that.

In the next several chapters we will explore the reasons why young people have sex. Craig and Drew show the first reason: they will have sex because they can. Here are parts of two letters young people wrote to me to explain why young people have sex:

> One of the reasons young people have sex is just to see what it is like. They hear about it in popular songs. They read about

it in books and magazines. They watch it in movies and on television. So they decide to try it out for themselves.

* * * * *

The movies and television shows and the lives of famous people show sex as something wonderful. It is no surprise that young people get interested. "What does it feel like?" "Is it really as great as they say?" When young people start to think about those questions, they are going to try to find the answers.

Young people want to learn about things they do not know, including sex. If they have a good understanding of the Bible's teaching about sex, they do not have to experiment on their own.

A Body Prepared for Sex

As children grow older, their bodies begin to change to prepare them to have children. For girls those changes can begin as early as 8 years old.[1] For boys it is about two years later. Those changes have a powerful influence on how the young person sees himself. They also have a strong influence on how boys think about girls and girls think about boys.

By the time young people are 14, the bodies of most of them are prepared to have children. That is much younger than was the case a hundred years ago. At the same time, marriage is delayed because of the increasing demands for more education. As a result, young people who save sex for marriage have to wait a much longer time than their grandparents did.

Young people today know much more about sex than their grandparents did. Sex is talked about freely and even shown in the media. They can go on the Internet and find anything they want to know. But they are not prepared emotionally to deal with sexual relationships. That preparation cannot be learned in school. It can be learned only in a loving relationship with adults who are fully developed emotionally. But those relationships are all too often missing from the American family.

Early Dating, Early Sex

Young people develop quickly. Each year that a young person waits before dating will help him or her be better prepared for that experience. Studies show that 91 percent of all girls who start dating at age 12 have sex by the time they are 18. Only 20 percent of girls who start dating at age 16 have sex by the time they are 18.[2]

Young people who are 12 or 13 do not start dating with the idea of having sex. But dating brings a boy and a girl closer together emotionally. That closeness leads to touching. Touching leads to sex. Then all they need is a time and a place where they can be alone. That can be found, for example, at the girl's house after school and before her parents get home from work. In one study both boys and girls who said they were sexually experienced had sex for the first time when they were 15.[3]

Alcohol, Drugs and Sex

People under the influence of alcohol or drugs do things they would not do if they were not under those influences. They lose some control over their actions because they cannot think clearly or make good decisions. This is especially true of young people. A 1998 study showed that young people who use alcohol or drugs are more likely to have sex than those who do not.[4]

A group at Columbia University examined material on 34,000 American young people. They talked with more than a hundred specialists on alcohol and drug use. They examined hundreds of studies on the use of alcohol, drugs and sex by young people.

They found that "63 percent of young people who use alcohol and 70 percent of young people who use it often have had sex. Only 26 percent of those who never drink alcohol have had sex."[5]

It is hard enough for young people to save sex until marriage. When alcohol and drugs are added, it becomes almost impossible. Their good judgment fails them, leaving them with pain and guilt and sorry for their actions.

The False Idea of Safe Sex

Craig and Drew's first date was at a party in their teacher's home. Drew's father took them and brought them home. They did not have even one minute to be together alone. But when Craig asked Drew to meet him at the Mall on Saturday, she agreed. There they went to a movie. In the dark theater Craig took Drew's hand, and she never let him go until the movie was finished. Over the next few months they spent much time together. As they found more and more time to be alone together, their touching and kissing increased.

The Saturday before Craig's fifteenth birthday Drew invited him to her house for a party. Her parents were gone for the weekend, and she did not invite any other young people. On the way there Craig stopped at a gas station and bought condoms from a machine in the restroom. He had heard that the use of a condom would remove the danger of an STD or a pregnancy. Drew served hamburgers, a birthday cake and wine coolers. The coolers were so good they each had two.

When Drew learned that Craig had condoms in his pocket, she cried out with excitement. The expectation Craig felt along with the alcohol from the wine coolers made it hard to get the condom in place. But he did it, and they had sex for the first time.

The idea that condoms provide safe sex has given our young people a false sense of security. While the use of condoms has increased, STDs have increased also. Not only do we see all the old STDs, but we see new and stronger ones as well.

A report from the Medical Institute for Sexual Health said that "safe sex" education is not working. "Clearly a change is needed to stop the current flood of STDs." The report said that while condoms are said to provide for safe sex, they fail about 2 percent to 4 percent of the time. Other studies have found an even higher rate of failure.[6] Besides, some STDs can be passed along even when condoms are used correctly every time.

We will look at the false idea of safe sex more fully later. Our point here is that the false idea of safe sex is one reason why young people do not wait for sex.

"If It Feels Good, Do It"

We know that sex feels good. It feels good for a husband and wife. It also feels good for any two people even if they are not married to each other. That is another reason why young people become sexually active. Here is what some young people have told me about the fun of sex:

> To most young people, sex is really not important. So they go ahead and have it just because they like it.

* * * * *

I used to know a boy who had sex many times and saw nothing wrong with it. One day I asked him what he did that weekend. He said he had a girl over to his place. I asked if his mother knew about it. He said, "No, she was out of town." Then I asked if he saw anything wrong with what he did. He said, "No. If it feels good, do it."

* * * * *

Many of my friends, both boys and girls, have sex because they just want to do it. When I ask them why, they say it makes them feel good.

* * * * *

Sex is fun and does not cost much. Having sex is one date that costs very little money and can be done almost anywhere. Life is empty anyway, so go for it!

Not only is sex fun, it brings two people closer together. God made sex that way for marriage, but it works outside of marriage also. Many of our young people are choosing to forget the things they have believed in order to enjoy sex before marriage.

Why do young people do that? In order to answer that question, we must examine our society's desire for fun. We live in a fallen world. There is so much pain and suffering in life. But no one likes to suffer, so we try to ease the pain. One of the ways we try to do that is by doing things that make us feel good. So people say, "If it feels good, do it" or "It cannot be wrong if it feels so right."

Our young people have accepted that way of thinking. That is one reason why they are not waiting until marriage to have sex. Sex helps them escape from the pain in their lives.

If you asked Craig or Drew what made them have sex, they might say, "We could not help it. The feelings were too strong to control." Like many other young people they do not understand that sex can be controlled. We are not just animals who must follow our desires without thinking. We are created in the likeness of God. We are thinking beings. Our actions should be under the control of our thinking.

Love – true love – is not just a feeling. It is an act of the will. It chooses to make the good and happiness of another person more important than our own. Since sex is an act of love, it should come as a result of a choice, not just of a desire that cannot be controlled. To say that sex is only an uncontrollable desire is to deny our ability to make choices. Young people need to understand that we can say no to sex.

Escape from the Demands of Life

Our young people have to meet many demands in life. Parents often do not understand how great those demands can be. When those demands begin to grow, sex provides an escape for a short time at least. Those demands are real, and the escape through sex is real. Sex does not solve the problem, but it does provide a short escape.

The desire to escape from the demands of life through sex is a sign that the person is not yet grown up. The body may seem grown up, but the mind and the emotions are not. A grown-up person shows self-control. A grown-up person deals with demands without seeking a short-term escape through such things as sex, alcohol or drugs. A grown-up person has a clear set of beliefs that directs his life even when the demands of life are great.

Sexually active young people may blame their actions on the demands of life. But they are still responsible for those actions. They cannot control the demands life makes on them, but they can control themselves. When young people are able to deal with the demands of life through self-control, they will not need to seek escape through sex.

One Thing Leads to Another

Closeness between a boy and a girl is like a drug. The more they get, the more they want. They always need more in order to reach the same level of satisfaction. First it is holding hands. Then it is kissing. Then the kisses become longer and deeper. Next is the touching of each other's body. Finally they have sex.

Once a boy and girl start having sex, that becomes the center of their relationship. The things they used to do together become unimportant. Then every trouble or disagreement they have is settled by having sex. When that no longer meets the need, the relationship falls apart.

It does not have to go that far, though. It is possible for a young person to stop, as one Christian girl explained to me in her letter:

> I felt pressed to have sex when I was dating Mike. My parents had always taught me the right way to live. I knew right from wrong. So it was not too hard to do what was right. At least it was not until Mike and I had been dating for two years. By then we were sure we were in love.

> One night he started feeling me in a way he never had before. That made me uneasy, but I enjoyed it too. After that things got more and more involved. One night Mike told me he wanted to show how much he loved me by having sex. I could not believe it! I just sat there for several minutes. I was shocked. I knew that what he wanted to do was wrong. I told him I could not do that and disappoint my parents.

Wanting a Child

Most young people who become sexually active have a great fear of becoming pregnant. Some girls, though, want to get pregnant. They feel so unloved. They want a baby to love and to love them in return. Other girls hope to get pregnant in order to force the boy to marry them. Such girls are not ready to be mothers.

Earlier Sexual Mistreatment

Many young people, especially girls, have been sexually misused by someone older than themselves. These young people are more likely to become sexually active at a younger age. That raises their chances of getting an STD. A 1996 study found that 10 percent of girls under the age of 18 had been sexually misused. These girls had sex with more men in the past year than had other girls who had not been sexually misused.[7]

Young people are children in grown-up bodies. We must help them get safely through this part of their lives so that they can be healthy and happy grown-ups later.

Chapter 5

Growing Up in a World Where Wrong Is Right

When I was growing up, most of the people I knew said that sex outside of marriage was wrong. My parents and my church said, "It is sin; do not do it." The radio and television said, "It is wrong; do not do it." The teachers at my public school agreed. Even most of the young people I knew said, "Do not do it." Certainly there were people who did "do it." But even they knew that most people believed it was wrong.

Things have changed. Our society no longer thinks about sex as it did then. Christian parents may still tell their children, "It is sin; do not do it." If the pastor says anything about sex at all, he may say, "It is sin; do not do it." But most school teachers say, "If you are going to do it, do it safely." The media and friends say, "It is fun; do it." So young people are strongly tempted to do it.

Many things in our culture affect how young people think and act. If young people are going to be able to say no to sex before marriage, they will have to understand our culture. The more they understand how the culture affects them, the better they will be able to wait until marriage.

In this chapter we will first examine how our culture disagrees with the teachings of the Bible about sex. Then we will look at some of the false ideas about sex that young people learn from the culture.

The Values of the Bible or the Values of Our Culture

Our culture has turned away from the values of the Bible. It no longer believes that it is possible to know what is right and what is wrong. It says that each person can decide for himself what is right for him. If he thinks it is right for him, it is right. But what is right for him may not be right for another person. What is right for him today may not be right for him tomorrow. What is right for him in his present situation may not be right for him if that situation changes.

Here is the problem. The new culture and the culture of the Bible often exist in the same home or the same church. Many adults still believe that the Bible is the final word on right and wrong. But most young people and many other adults accept the new culture. We are not experiencing a difference between older people and younger people. We are experiencing a difference between the teachings of the Bible and a set of ideas that are very different from the Bible.

Today's Christian young people are growing up in two cultures at the same time. We cannot just say, "Sex outside of marriage is sin; do not do it." Young people want to know why it is sin. Adults must answer their questions.

Young people have always felt that their parents did not understand them or the world in which they lived. But that sense of misunderstanding has never been as great as it is today. If parents do not understand that difference, they may never be able to talk with their young people. They may never be able to lead their young people in God's way.

Christian parents and the church must give clear teaching about the truths of the Bible. Only in that way will young people be prepared to stand against an un-Christian culture.

A Culture Without Purpose

In the new culture, young people have nothing to guide them. But they need someone to tell them what is right and what is wrong. Here is how two young people put it:

46

Most young people really want some rules and direction. If you ask a boy if he wants rules, he will probably laugh at you. Deep down inside, though, he wants someone to say, "Stop! Do not do that." Yet, for many young people, no one ever does.

* * * * *

Young people today do not know what to think. Nearly every relationship leaves them feeling betrayed. They ask themselves, "Whom can I trust?" Young people have rebelled against rules in the past, but they always had a cause. Today's young people have no cause. We have just given up.

Today's young people do not know what to think about life. They are given plenty of information. Then they are told that there is no such thing as truth. They are taught that man is no more than an animal. Then they are told that they should feel good about themselves.

People no longer want to accept the Bible, but without the Bible there is no way to tell right from wrong. So people give up trying to decide what is right and what is wrong and do whatever they want to do. That leads to feelings of emptiness. People try to fill that emptiness with fun.

Young people need to know how to tell right from wrong. They need to see adults who live by what is right.

Sex in a Sinful Culture

Today's young people are growing up in a culture that expects them to be sexually active. Dr. Ruth is a famous teacher about sex. She says that if a boy and a girl want to have sex they should do so. Their desire for sex is too strong for them to wait. But if the boy wants to have sex and the girl does not, he should wait. This is the kind of foolish teaching young people are getting. If the boy can wait if the girl does not want to have sex, they can both wait even if they both want to have sex.

The truth is that young people will act the way the culture expects them to act. If the culture expects them to have sex, they will have sex. If the culture expects them to wait, most of them will wait.

Our Self-centered Culture

Pleasing one's self has become the most important thing in our culture. That has greatly changed the way young people think and act. A hundred years ago a young girl in America who wanted to be better might have promised herself:

> I will no longer talk about myself or my feelings. I will think before speaking. I will hold back myself in talking with other people and in my actions. I will listen when people talk to me. I will be more grown up in my actions. I will take a greater interest in other people.

Today a young girl in America who wants to be better might promise herself:

> I will use any money I get to make myself look better. I will lose weight and get new eyeglasses. I will get a different haircut, different clothes and the things to go with them. I will get new makeup.[1]

We might hope that Christian young people would not be influenced by the culture's concern with self. But that is not true. Even if they hold to Christian teachings about sex, they find a way to make sex seem right. One way they do that is by making "love" mean the same thing as marriage. If they really love someone, they say, that is the same as being married.

48

Lost in the Culture

Americans move often. When they move they do not get to know the people who live near them. A friend once told me that he read in the newspaper about a boy who died in a car accident. The boy was the son of the family that lived across the street from him. Before he read about the accident in the newspaper, he did not even know the name of the family or that they had a son.

Relationships that mean anything take time to develop. Many young people today have never lived in one place very long. They have never had the chance to develop the relationships that would help them deal with the problems of life.

Another problem is that young people are growing up with so much uncertainty. They do not know how to prepare to live in a world that is changing so quickly. The job they are training for may not even exist when they finish their training. With such empty hopes for the future, many young people want to take all they can get in the present. *Why wait for sex*, they wonder, *if tomorrow may never come.*

Lies Our Culture Tells

Our culture has its own beliefs about sex before marriage. Many of these beliefs are not true. But young people accept them and make their decisions about sex based on them.

"No One Will Get Hurt"

Young people have accepted the belief that "no one will get hurt" by sex before marriage. They believe they have the right to do what they want with their own bodies. They think that if they are careful they will not get pregnant or get an STD.

49

There are two problems with that way of thinking. First, they are closing their eyes to all the pain sex before marriage has caused for other people. They can see that pain among their friends. They can read about it in the newspapers. There is the pain of STDs, pregnancies and broken relationships.

Second, they are accepting the thinking of the sinful culture instead of God's absolute rules of right and wrong. God's rules for sex are for all people, in all times and in all situations.

"It Is All Right Since We Are Going to Get Married"

Many young people think the promise of marriage is the same as being married. That was what Lori and Jeff thought. A student wrote to me about what happened to them:

> Lori and Jeff were strong Christians. They had been dating for seven months when they fell into the trap of the enemy. Lori explained, "I thought it would not be bad to have sex because we knew we were going to be married." She forgot that God does not look at future promises when dealing with present sin.

> Satan will try to make you think that if you really love someone God understands your need to express that love by having sex. That is not true. After a time of being sexually active, Lori and Jeff started having trouble. That trouble continued for two months. It could have destroyed their relationship. They repented of their actions, but the marks of the wounds are still there. Lori talks of the time when they were "involved in sin." "Our prayer life suffered," she said, "and so did other things. I thought, 'Now Jeff is coming to see me for just one thing.'"

Studies show that half the people who get married had planned to marry at least one other person before. So planning to get married does not mean that you will marry that person.[2]

50

Another study shows that 78 percent of people who get divorced had sex before marriage. They also were more likely to have sex with a person other than their husband or wife while they were married.

Here is part of a letter written by a Christian leader to a young woman about to be married. In it he tells about the experience of a girl named Pat:

Pat first had sex when she was 16. She became a Christian a year later. As a Christian she learned that sex before marriage is wrong, but she found it hard to stop. Finally Pat decided to stop dating boys until she was stronger spiritually. During that time she really grew in her spiritual life.

About two years later Bill asked her for a date. He was a Christian and one of the leaders in her church. Since she was so much stronger than she had been, she agreed to date Bill. After that first date, they continued to date. Bill was always very careful with her, and Pat felt safe with him. He even asked her before he kissed her the first time.

As they spent more and more time together, their kisses became longer and longer. Then one evening Bill started exploring her body with his hands. Later he said he was sorry and promised that it would never happen again. But it did happen again and kept on happening. One night he went too far, and she stopped him. He could see that she was angry with him. Again he said he was sorry and explained that he was only trying to give her enjoyment. She told him she did not want that kind of enjoyment – not yet at least.

They talked about why she did not want him to do what he was doing. But he never seemed to really understand her or remember what she had said. They would pray together and promise each other that it would never happen again. But it did happen again and again.

She told me, "If it was happening to another woman, I would advise her to get out of the relationship. But how do you get out of a relationship when it is with someone you want to spend the rest of your life with?"

We talked again about two months later. "I understand now that my relationship with Bill is very different from the relationships I was in when I was younger. Bill and I are really in love, and we plan to be married in about three months. What we are doing now will prepare us for our wedding night. That will make our marriage stronger."

During that time Pat's spiritual life suffered. She stopped praying and reading her Bible. She lost interest in church. Before she and Bill became sexually involved, she was such a happy Christian. Now she seemed sad most of the time. She often became angry, even with Bill. Maybe especially with Bill.

Pat and Bill never did marry. Pat finally admitted that it was their sexual activity that was the problem. She said, "As I look back, I know that it was our sexual activities that were deadly. We could no longer think well of each other. We felt guilty. And I was always angry, angry at myself but also angry at Bill."

Pat thought that her relationship with Bill was different and that made it right. It was not right, though, because it was against the teaching of God's Word. She thought that they would certainly get married later, but they never did.

"I Owe It to Him"

If a girl thinks she owes a boy sex, it is because he wants her to think that. He is thinking only about himself. He only wants to "use" her. In the Christian way of looking at life, though, we do not "use" people.

A girl who has sex with a boy because she "owes it to him" is selling her body. She is giving him what he wants so that he will give her what she wants. She may not want sex, but whatever it is she does want she hopes he will give it to her. Perhaps she only wants to feel that someone loves her. Perhaps she wants to feel desirable. Sex, though, is not something to be bought and sold.

The boy who makes a girl feel that she owes him sex does not want sex with her especially. He just wants sex. He wants to take, not to give. A girl who is willing to give on those conditions does not think very well of herself.

"Prove Your Love by Having Sex"

Many boys ask a girl to have sex "to prove your love." Even if the girl does not want to have sex, she may do so. That is true even of Christian girls. They are made to believe that love is the same as marriage. If sex is made for marriage and love is the same as marriage, then they should show their love by having sex.

When the Bible talks about true love, though, it always means words and actions that lead the other person closer to God. Nowhere in the Bible does love lead another person into sin. Sex without marriage can never show true love. It can never show the love of God.

"Sex Proves That I Am Grown Up"

Young people are children who are growing into adults. They become adults in some ways before they do in other ways. Their bodies are able to have sex before their minds and emotions are ready. They are not yet fully able to tell right from wrong. They are not yet able to stand up for what they believe to be right. They cannot see the price they may have to pay for their actions. Just having an adult body does not make a person an adult.

A man who works with young people told me:

> High school girls try to act like married people. One way
> they do that is by having sex. For many years they have
> dreamed about being married. Now they want to play like
> they are married. But I have heard them say that when they
> had sex they gave away their youth. They were sorry about
> that. They were especially sorry if they got pregnant.

"Once You Have Had Sex, There Is No Turning Back"

Young people believe that once they become sexually active there
is no reason to stop. They have already lost their innocence and
they can never get that back, they say. A Christian who accepts
that kind of thinking has given up on God's forgiveness. But
God's forgiveness is never-ending.

Whatever our sin, God offers us the chance to leave the
old ways behind and begin to live His way. That can start
anytime we choose. If we have taken ten steps away from
God, He has already taken nine steps toward us. But we
have to take that last step to have again the relationship with
Him that we gave away.

Just two things are needed for us to get back into relationship with
God: repentance and forgiveness. In repentance we agree with
God that we have sinned and tell Him that we never want to do it
again. Then God forgives and accepts us as though we had never
sinned. He can do that only because Christ died for our sins.

When we agree with God about our sin and accept His forgiveness,
we are able to start over again. To say that God cannot or will not
forgive is to say that His grace is not able to cover our sin. That
hurts Him more than any other thing we could do.

If a young person chooses to continue in sex before marriage,
there is great danger. There are all kinds of traps waiting for

such a young person. The longer he or she stays sexually active, the less likely he or she is to escape without harm. There is the danger of STDs and pregnancies. There is also danger of damaged emotions, ruined relationships and guilt. Some of those conditions will stay with the young person for life.

* * * * *

Today's culture is telling young people, "Enjoy sex now. It is foolish to wait." Perhaps the loudest voice is that of the media. In the next chapter we will examine how the media is giving young people other strong reasons not to wait for sex.

Chapter 6
The Media's Influence

Remember Derek from Chapter 1? He is a Christian student who is wondering about the question, "Why should true love wait?" A talk he had with his friend Colin first made him think about that question. Here is a little more about Derek. He and Colin enjoy going to movies. Watching someone save the world all by himself is a welcome change from the pressures of Derek's studies.

Derek does not watch movies that make sex sin seem right. He is careful about what he watches because he knows he can be strongly influenced by sex movies. He likes to watch what is called action movies. Even those sometimes give a quick look at a woman's bare skin. Usually they include a sex act or two. Derek wishes the makers of the movies would not do that, but it does not really affect him. Or does it?

Here is a little more about Annie, the Christian girl who has started dating Jeff, a young soldier.

To escape the pressures of school and work, she reads love stories. Most of the time she reads about a hero and his girlfriend getting closer to God. They never get into bed with each other before marriage. Sometimes she reads a story where the hero and his girlfriend do not always do the right thing. But everything turns out fine by the end of the story. Annie says their bad actions are because they were not Christians at first. Such stories have not hurt her. Or have they?

Young people are growing up in a world where the media are always present. The media are always trying to tell us something or sell us something. About sex, the media mostly tell lies.

In "Why Wait for Sex?" for Inter-Varsity Christian Fellowship, Alice Fryling wrote:

Our world is starved for closeness. Many of the lies we believe have to do with our hunger to be close to another person. We believe that sex will satisfy that hunger. We want to be loved, touched and understood in a world where family closeness is becoming a thing of the past. These desires are as old as people. What is different today is that people are trying to satisfy these desires in unusual ways.[1]

What Are the Media Trying to Sell?

Daily we hear about sex from the media. Sex is used to sell everything from cars to clothes. Television, movies, books and newspapers urge us to experiment with sex without thought of the cost.

Programs just for enjoyment influence young people even more than messages to sell something do. To show this, here is a part of a letter I received from a girl in West Virginia:

> I accepted Jesus as my Savior when I was 9. I had been going to church all my life and still do. At age 17 I began dating a boy who had finished school and gotten a job at a factory in town. I thought he was wonderful. Well, one night we went to see a sexy movie. On the way home we had sex in the back seat of his mother's car. After five months of dating, he left me. I was crushed.

This story is being repeated in the lives of many young people. One of the main reasons behind this sad fact is the lies the media tell young people about sex. What are those lies? Abbylin Sellers gives six media lies about sex. For each lie Sellers gives us the true message young people need to learn.

Lie 1: Sex creates closeness. True closeness is built on the promise to be honest and loving.

Lie 2: Starting sex early will help you get to know one another and have a better relationship later. Sex is an art that is learned best in the safe environment of marriage.

Lie 3: Sex without a long-term promise is fun and gives you a sense of freedom. A satisfying sexual relationship needs trust that grows only in a marriage that lasts a lifetime.

Lie 4: If you do not express your sex freely, you must be crushing your sexual desire. Maybe there is something wrong with you. Maybe you are letting other people control your life. This lie can frighten you. The fact is that sex before marriage is bad for you in many ways.

Lie 5: Sex is freedom. No one is really free who takes part in an activity just because others are doing it.

Lie 6: Surely God understands that these are modern times. God did not give rules because He did not want us to enjoy life. Just the opposite is true about sex. Because He is God and loves us so much, He has told us how to have the best sexual experiences. That is in marriage.[2]

Television

Television is a great influence in the daily experience of our families. Americans spend about one-third of their free time watching television.[3] Television often has a bad influence on our actions. Young people who watch television the most do more poorly in school.[4] Young people who are sexually active watch television more than those who are not sexually active.[5]

In the early evening, when most people are watching, television shows about three sexual acts each hour.[6] Girls watch more television with sex in it than boys do.[7] Pregnant girls watch more television than those who are not pregnant.[8] Most of the sex on television is talk, not naked people;[9] but 10 percent of all programs show or talk about the sex act.[10]

In one study older boys and girls who saw a large number of sexual acts on television were more likely to believe that others their age did those things too.[11] Many young people agree with what this girl wrote:

When I was young, I watched adult stories on television every day. What a mistake it is to fill the young mind with such thinking! I also purchased sex-filled reading at a very young age. My mother did not care what I read. Thoughts of sexual acts were fixed in my mind during a very serious time in my young life. By the eighth grade I was already touching and kissing boys during playtime. This continued during high school. When I went away to school, I began having sex.

Not everything seen on television is make-believe. Young people see that girls who act for television have children before marriage. Those girls seem to have wonderful lives. In this way television seems to say that sex outside of marriage is right much more often than it says it is wrong. No wonder young people go out and experiment with sex.

Music

Here is what some young people say about music:

Another reason young people have sex before marriage is the music they listen to. The words in rock music and country music talk freely about sex. Many songs talk of "one-night lovers" or "part-time lovers."

* * * * *

Some young people may say, "Oh, I do not listen to the words. I just like the music." But they do hear the words, and they learn them. Then they may begin to think that any kind of sex is all right. That is not good.

* * * * *

Over Christmas, my brother tried to make me angry by calling a sexy song a great song. Calling a sexy song great leads young people into having sex without even questioning it.

When music that young people like talks so much about sex, it is no surprise that they are affected by it. Abraham Maslow studied the "biggest experiences" in human lives. Experiences that involved music were number two on his list. The number one experience was sex. Imagine then how sex and music together really are powerful.

Frank Zappa wrote that rock music is sex. The big beat matches the body's beat, and the words of the song strengthen it. If a young person chooses to listen to music that tears people down instead of building them up, he shows which influences he wants to shape his life.

Pornography

The most damaging lies the media tell about sex are about pornography. Pornography is using words or pictures to excite sexual desire. It leads to the most harmful kinds of sex. One of the most popular ways to find pornography is on the Internet. Young people use their home computers to find sexual material of every kind. In chapter 18 we will share some ways for adults to help young people escape this danger.

The Media's Biggest Lie

Hardly anyone seen on television or in the movies pays a price for wrong sex. But in real life, people often pay a high price. A number of studies show that the media is lying about the dangers of wrong sex. One report says that sex shows up in 75 percent of programs during the time when children are watching the most. Only one in 10 of these programs talks about the dangers and responsibilities of sex.

Another study showed that 156 sex acts were shown in 50 hours of television. The only mention of HIV/AIDS was that it came through drug use, not through sexual actions.[12] Another study said that only 10 percent of the shows studied talked of any possible results of having sex, such as unplanned pregnancy.[13] No show talked about how sex outside of marriage can lead to AIDS or the judgment of God.

When Derek sees sex between two unmarried people in a war movie, he may consider it innocent and harmless. The two people enjoy themselves and then go on with their lives. Derek is left with the idea that sex before marriage is not so bad.

That is not real life, though. It is make-believe. It is a lie. In real life, people often end up with disease or death. No wonder Derek has begun to question God's rules on sex before marriage. He is being influenced by the lie.

The last love story Annie read ended with a young woman in the arms of a nice-looking man. He had just led her into the joys of sex. But books like that hardly ever tell the results many young women suffer after giving in to a man and then being left alone. So when Annie's boyfriend excites her with loving words, what reason does she give for saying no to sex?

Our actions are the result of our thoughts. Our thoughts are the result of what we put into our minds. The longer and harder we think on these thoughts, the more likely we will be to act them out.

When our thoughts do not agree with the truth, our actions will not agree with the truth either.

As a person thinks, so he is, say the Scriptures (Proverbs 23:7). That is why the Bible tells us to guard our hearts, or minds (Proverbs 4:23). We should not open ourselves up to temptation (Matthew 6:13). We should want to be like God, not like the world (Romans 12:1-2; I John 2:15).

The Lie of False Values

What are the results of the media's lies? Young people are getting thousands of messages that sex outside of marriage is harmless. So every year millions of young people are getting pregnant or getting STDs. The media does little to show right values or the results of wrong values.

The current fear about the spread of AIDS, however, has brought some signs of change. The media seem to be saying that it is safer to have sex with only one person. The media also are showing more concern for the safety of both persons. However, the way the media are leading will only result in more sex outside of marriage. It will not produce a godly way of thinking about sex or of true love.

The media show young people that the cure for everything is to jump into bed with another person. The concerned parent says, "Wait, have no sex." No wonder there are problems.

The media say that the value of a person is mostly the beauty of his or her body. How the media explains that beauty, though, is always changing. The media have such power over young people because of the time they spend listening, watching and reading.

As a result young people spend less time with older people. They end up believing and acting out the lies the media tell.

The Scriptures warn us to flee the sinful things young people want to do (2 Timothy 2:22). If a young person knows this and still has sex outside of marriage, he or she is to blame for the results.

One young woman wrote to me about the high price she paid for sex sin:

> What the movies and the television do not tell us is the pain and the broken hearts that come from sex outside of marriage. I cannot treat these things as though they were unimportant. The hardest thing I have ever gone through is getting over my relationship with a married man. It was harder than having surgery. It was harder than being tested for cancer. It was harder than a broken marriage. It was harder than losing one job after another. It was the most painful thing I have ever had to do.

Putting the Media in Its Place

The thoughts of young people about sex must change. For that to happen, either the media must change or the listening and watching habits of young people must change. Young people must learn how to choose what to watch or read or listen to. They must learn to use the Bible in making those choices.

The best influence young people can have is godly parents. Parents themselves must understand God's teaching about sex and be able to teach those things to their young people. They will not be able to do that, though, unless they have a good relationship with their young people. That relationship must be built when those young people are still small children.

The Bible tells parents to teach their children God's commands (Deuteronomy 6:6-7; Ephesians 6:4). The more young people are taught from their early years to choose right, the easier it will be for them to do right when temptation comes.

Young people are looking for something to fill their deepest needs, such as love and acceptance. Those needs were put in them by God. They should be met through the home, the church and the school. When they are not met there, young people will try to meet them in some other way. In the next chapter we will explore how some of the important adults in a child's life are a big part of the problem.

Chapter 7
A "Love Hunger" at Home

Students at some schools are known for their unkindness toward visiting speakers, especially Christian speakers. As I waited for my turn to speak at one of those schools, I was a little concerned. Would they be interested in what I had to say? Would they listen?

As I stepped up to speak, the students were very noisy. So I spoke extra loudly. I said, "Almost everyone of you has two fears. One, you are afraid you will never be loved. Two, you are afraid you will never be able to love."

Immediately they were very quiet. They wanted to hear what I was going to say next. Most students do have these two deep fears. Many doctors believe that this hunger for love is one reason many young people have sex before they marry.

In this chapter we will look at two ways a hunger for love in the home can lead to sex before marriage. First we will look at the lack of parents' love and example. Then we will look at the lack of parents' teaching about sex.

The Lack of Parents' Love and Example

God planned that parents' love for each other should be an example to their children. If young people learn love at home, they will not have to look for it some other place.

When love between a father and a mother breaks down, children do not learn how to give or receive love. Young people who grow up with a hunger for love at home are afraid they will never find it. So they often will have sexual experiences. These will only make their pain and hunger for love greater. After listening to one of my talks in England, a 16-year-old wrote to me, "I wish someone would just love me and show me they care."

65

Where sex before marriage is concerned, the only answer is to stop it before it starts. This begins with parents spending time with their children. This should start long before their children begin to feel the pressures to have sex.

The Example of Parents

The greatest reason why young people get involved in sex is that their parents do not show enough interest in them. A study shows that nearly one in three parents does not seriously show an interest in the life of their young people. That is especially true about that young person's time at school.[1]

Parents who do not show an interest in their children cause a hunger for love in both parents and children. Parents who have a hunger for love raise children who have an even greater hunger for love. That leads to terrible results.

When a young person feels connected to his family and his parents are involved in his life, he is protected. Young people are also protected by their parents being with them at important times during the day. Those important times are in the morning, after school, at dinner and at bedtime. Children are also protected by their parents expecting them to do well in school. Loving parents who give a clear message about delaying sex have children who are less likely to have sex before marriage.[2]

Young people are crying out for parents who are good examples of love, marriage, sex and family. One of the greatest things parents can do for their children is to love each other and let their children know it.

Searching for a Father's Love

Even though love from both parents is important, most young people especially want love from their fathers. One reason for this is that men have problems with showing their emotions. A story written by a young woman shows the great importance of a father's love:

When I was 14, I dated an 18-year-old boy. After a month or so, he told me that he loved me. He said if I loved him I would have sex with him. If I would not, he said he would have to leave me. I knew sex before marriage was wrong, but I so wanted to have a man love me.

I was not sure of my father's love. I always felt that I had to earn it. So, here was my boyfriend. He was telling me he loved me. I needed that love. If the condition to keep that love was to have sex with him, I felt I had to do it. I knew it was wrong, but I did not want to lose the man who loved me. So I gave in.

After two years my boyfriend and I separated. Then I started doing the same thing with other men. I wanted so much to find someone who would love me without having sex. But every man I dated said, "If you love me, you will have sex." At the age of 21, I finally found a Man who really loved me.

The young woman found Jesus, who gave His love without conditions. She tells about when she met Jesus:

I felt so lonely tonight, just one of many times I have felt that way. I finally understood that I was lonely for a father. I wanted to be able to call him when I hurt, have him listen to me, hear him say he understands. I never had that with my father.

Yet tonight God spoke to me in a quiet way and said He was there for me. I said, "Will You be my father? Yes, I know You will. And the most wonderful thing about You as my father is that I can be with You all the time."

One study found that 72 percent of women want to be held closely and treated gently more than they want to have sex.[3] I often receive letters from young people like these girls:

> You made me cry today when you talked at my high school about your relationship with your daughter. I wish someone loved me like you love your family.

* * * * *

> My mother has been married two times. Neither husband was a father to me. You said that most young people do not want to have sex, they just want someone to care. That is so true! I have almost fallen into the "sex trap" because I just wanted a man to love me.

Perhaps some of you fathers are feeling that I am not being fair. Yes, there are mothers who do not attend well to their children. But I think we men must take much of the blame for our young people being what they are.

Broken Families

There are many divorces in our world today. Young people fear that it will happen to their parents or they feel the pain of a family already hurt by divorce. This causes them to reach out for sex in place of the love of their parents. I learned about this fear many years ago from my own son, Sean, who was only 6 years old. He came home from school a little sad. I asked what was wrong. "Nothing," he said.

Because we got along well together, I said, "Come on, tell me why you are sad."

He waited a little and then asked, "Are you going to leave Mother?" Three of his friends' fathers had just divorced their mothers, and Sean was afraid I might do the same.

I sat down with Sean. "I want you to know one thing," I said. "I love your mother very much. I will never leave her."

That little 6-year-old smiled at me and said, "Thanks." He was not looking for love for himself. He needed the security that comes from knowing that his mother and I love each other and plan a permanent marriage. All young people need to be part of a permanent marriage.

Most young people feel that it is too easy to get a divorce. Of young people from divorced homes, most said their parents did not try hard enough. One reason divorce is so damaging to young people is that they no longer see their fathers every day.

Divorce

Divorce has a greater effect on a child than the death of a parent. There are several reasons why that is true. First, when children lose a parent through death, they usually do not feel that they are responsible for the death. When they lose a parent through divorce, they often blame themselves.

A boy of 10 said to me in all seriousness, "If had kept my room clean, my father would not have left my mother." He said his father used to criticize him because his room was always dirty. When his parents separated, the boy thought it was because he did not keep his room clean.

I talked with a young woman whose parents were divorced when she was 16. She said, "If I had been a better cook, my father would never have divorced by mother." Because her mother worked outside the home, Debbie was responsible to prepare the evening meals. Her father often criticized her cooking. Then one night he just left. Seven years later, Debbie still said, "My father divorced my mother because I was a bad cook."

The second reason it is more difficult to lose a parent through divorce than through death is that in divorce there is never a final end. When a parent dies, it is painful; but the child later understands mother or father is gone. After a period of mourning, he goes on with his life. There is no ending with divorce. It just goes on and on.

I hear so many divorced parents say, "My children really handled the divorce well." On the outside children may seem to be doing well, but they are hurting inside. Divorce is a main reason our children lose hope. That may cause them to start looking for love in all the wrong places.

Broken Home, Broken Children

When God made man in His own likeness, He did not just make a man. He made a woman also. Although each person is made like God, the complete likeness of God is shown in the marriage of a man and a woman. When that marriage is broken, the likeness of God in the home is broken.

Earthly fathers are to point their families to the heavenly Father. That is God's plan, yet the family as God planned it has almost disappeared from America in recent years. We are seeing many effects of this on our children. One of those effects is being involved in early sex.

Broken homes can lead to sex before marriage in at least four ways. One is the lack of values that results from such a divided family. Children are taught that they should be kind. Yet parents do not forgive each other.

A second reason a broken home can lead to sex before marriage is that the influence of other young people is stronger than that of the home. The closeness and sharing that should take place in the family is looked for in another person.

A third reason is that a lack of security in the home may cause a young person to look for closeness in wrong ways.

A fourth reason is the way divorce may make a child think of himself. Children of divorced parents feel rejected by their parents. Sex allows that young person to feel important and wanted by someone.

Children Need Clear Teaching About Sex

When love is missing from the home, there is not much helpful talk. Sex is not talked about and so learning about sex is not complete. What is learned may not even be true. Then young people think sex is a mystery. That makes them want to explore it.

The Kaiser Family Foundation says, "The more you teach a child about sex, the less likely he or she will be to have sex. Yet only 44 percent of parents have discussed sex with their child."[4]

Teaching about sex in an intelligent and open way must begin at home. Young people need to know that the changes in their bodies and the changing emotions that go with them are normal. They will find out some way how their bodies work. When parents and the church deny children the facts they need, they set their young people up for trouble. Learning about sex must begin at a very young age and continue as the child grows up.

Many parents do not understand how much influence they have on the sexual ideas of their children. A YMCA report shows that young people say that 80 percent of their sexual values comes from their parents.[5] That same study found that "not having enough time together" with their parents is the biggest concern among young people today.[6]

Young people really want to find the answers to their questions about sex at home. Parents need to really listen to what their young people are saying. If parents show an interest in their children when they are young, the children will show an interest in their parents later.

Teaching How Sex Fits into the Whole Plan of Life

A parent's most important job is to explain what part sex plays in God's whole plan for our lives. During health class at school, children may learn the way a baby is made. But they usually will not learn about God's plan for sex in their lives.

Young people need to know about both sex and love and how they are different. Every person has a God-given desire for love. When young people see love in their parents, they learn how to love. Too many children grow up learning from their parents that love means, "Get what you can from the other person. When that person does not act right, leave him or her." The children then get the idea that sex is the same as love.

Children grow up wanting to love their parents, but they may not be sure about their relationship. They try to act especially nice so that their parents will love them. If they do something they think will not please their parents, they hide it. If they think that being honest will disappoint their parents, they stop talking. Their whole idea of love is based on actions. Then when a boy says, "If you love me, you will have sex," the girl thinks she has to show her love.

The biblical picture of love is one of giving without expecting anything in return. It accepts another person without conditions. This is a security not based on actions. It is very different from the self-centered love being taught today.

Lack of Facts

God warns parents to teach their children biblical truths. That includes the truth about sex. If parents do not teach them, who will?

Although Western culture grew out of Christianity, it now attacks Christian ideas. If young people do not have Christian examples and teaching in the home, they will look outside the home. Without knowing God and His love, they settle for anything that looks like love, even if it hurts them.

Sex as an Expression of Rebellion

Children sometimes rebel against their parents, and sex is one way they rebel. It happens in homes where parents and children are usually in conflict. It also can happen when parents are doing their best to teach and be examples of biblical love and sex. Children write to me about rebellion. One wrote:

> People my age have sex because other young people pressure them or because they rebel against their parents. From what I see at my school, some parents do not care about their children. They do not care who they are with or what they are doing. The children rebel by doing something they think will harm their parents. They do not understand that they are harming themselves more than they are harming any other person.

Rebellion is usually caused by a lack of a good relationship. The rebellious child is reacting to a poor relationship between the parents and the child and between the parents themselves. One marriage and family adviser thinks that in as many as 95 percent of families who have a rebellious child, the parents need help in their marriage. He reports improvement in the children's actions when the parents' relationship improves.

Setting rules for a young person will not work if there is not a good relationship between him and the one making the rules. The child will rebel since he or she does not believe the one making the rules has the child's best interest at heart. When this happens, parents often lay down even more rules.

Concerned parents can take steps to repair the relationship with a rebellious child. First, parents need to remember that rules without a relationship leads to rebellion. Second, reduce the number of rules as much as possible. Let the children know you want to rebuild trust. Be careful, though, about allowing too much freedom. Bad relationships will not change immediately. Children will not change just because you expect them to change.

One of the most powerful ways to build a relationship is to listen. That shows that the child is important to you. As the relationship and trust are rebuilt, there will be less and less rebellion.

Chapter 8
Young People in Need Turn to Sex

Another reason young people do not wait until marriage for sex is that they are trying to meet emotional and relationship needs. In one study young people were asked, "Why do young people you know have sex?" Sixty-three percent of the girls and 50 percent of the boys answered, "They were in love."[1]

Most young people say they have been in love sometime in their lives. When they tell their parents, their parents say they are too young to know about love. But the young people still reach out for love in ways that really hurt them. A hurting girl told me the following story:

> I trusted Bobby to know how far we could go without having sex. He told me many times that he loved me. He was sure I did not love him as much as he loved me. It was then I had to prove that I was all his. The first time we had sex, I had no idea what was happening. After we did it, he just went to sleep. I felt so alone. I have never hated myself more. But it was too late then to do anything about it. Sex became an everyday thing. My only fear was losing Bobby. Even if he treated me badly I was going to do anything I could to keep him.

I loved him and he made me think he loved me, but he did not love me. It was a trick. Bobby's "love" was a selfish love, nothing like the love found in 1 Corinthians 13:4-7:

"Love does not give up. Love is kind. Love is not jealous. Love does not put itself up as being important. Love has no pride. Love does not do the wrong thing. Love never thinks of itself. Love does not get angry. Love does not remember the suffering that comes from being hurt by someone. Love is not happy with sin. Love is happy with the truth. Love takes everything that comes without giving up. Love believes all things. Love hopes for all things. Love keeps on in all things."

75

The Bible shows us what God's love is like. Remember what we said in chapter 1? Love makes the security and happiness of another as important to us as our own. That kind of love tries to guard and strengthen the honor God has given each person.

Many young people think of love as one of two things. They think it is a warm feeling or they think it is a relationship that makes them feel good. Both of these are self-centered and are the opposite of the Bible's idea of love. To many young people, "love" seems to be a good reason to have sex before marriage.

One large study found that 46 percent of Christian young people believe that if they truly love someone, it makes sex "right." These Christian young people surely do not understand the real meaning of love and the purpose of sex.[2] Another study found that girls who have had sex feel that love is the main reason. Only 25 percent of boys agree. Most boys, especially those who have had sex, will say, "I had sex because I could."[3]

The pressure to have sex makes the person feel that his willingness to have sex is the test of love. But sex is never a test of love. The true test of love is in how we treat people.

Usually the boy and girl discover later that what they thought was love was only sexual excitement. Now they must live with the results. The words "If you love me, you will have sex with me" should be answered as these young people did:

> If you love me, you will consider my feelings and not push me into doing something I am not ready for.

> OK, prove how you love me by understanding and considering my feelings.

> Love or no love, sex can result in a baby and that is important.

I love you. But I would feel better showing you in another way.

Many young people today are crying out for love so much that they will believe anything and go for anyone. The following story by Dr. L.R. Clark shows how far young people will go to get the love they seek:

Anitra was in the hospital with a serious health problem. She was 16 years old and had a 7-month-old baby. The baby's father was in jail. Anitra admitted that she had been trying to have another child with her new boyfriend. The truth was that she felt a child would make her boyfriend stay with her. I asked her about her desires for the future. With tears in her eyes, she said, "Without babies and men, what is there for me?"

Although I wanted to cry with her, I decided to do something more helpful. I asked her to make a list of things she had thought about but had never tried to do. The next day Anitra had a list of 15 things waiting for me. It included acting, singing and becoming a nurse or a lawyer. We then made a plan to help her begin some of those interests. Since leaving the hospital she has delayed her plans to have another baby. She has returned to her church. She is trying hard to make a future for herself and her child.[4]

Searching for Security and Self-Worth

A young person's search for security and self-worth often takes the form of sex before marriage. Consider these messages from young people:

Sins against God lead to terrible things. In the case of my girlfriend and me, sex hurt each of us and damaged our relationship with each other. Later it hurt others who were not a part of our relationship. I used sex to make me feel that

I was worth something. Each time I had sex I thought that it proved that I was accepted by at least one girl. I looked to sex to help my self-worth instead of looking for worth in the eyes of my Creator. When my girlfriend became pregnant, my self-worth went even lower.

* * * * *

Never think that getting what you want from someone is going to increase your sense of self-worth. The Word of God says, "He who wants to keep his life will have it taken away from him. He who loses his life because of Me will have it given back to him" (Matthew 10:39). I have found that basing my self-worth on anything apart from being accepted by God leaves me empty.

* * * * *

I had many sexual relationships, but the thing that hurt the most was the hatred that came out of those relationships later. Deep down inside I was not sure girls accepted me or that I was a man. The pressures were very strong. Sometimes I felt lonely if I did not get a girl when all my friends did.

A girl may not feel secure. She meets the "perfect man," but really this man is having the same problems she is having. Because neither one of them knows what real love is, they may mistake sex for love. That is where many people my age get into trouble.

God means for our personal needs to be met by Him and not by other people. In the past people could feel pretty secure within the family. But that is not true in most cases today. Now the family is often a place of unrest. Married people know they will be left alone if they do not please their husband or wife. Children growing up in that kind of situation lack security. That leaves them feeling worthless. They do not feel free to be themselves.

One way to develop the feeling of self-worth is to allow for the freedom to fail, the freedom not to be perfect. Such freedom can be present only when a person feels secure. That person feels accepted for who he is, not for what he does. Security like that is what young people need to develop in their relationships. When they do, it will help in their marriages.

When two people promise themselves to each other, they both have freedom. They do not need to put on a show to gain the other's approval. Then, when they are married, they have the security to be themselves, to admit what they do not know. They do not have to be experts at sex when they are first married because they both know it is their first time. Part of the excitement of beginning a life together is learning about sex together, guiding and helping each other. That is worth waiting for.

Apart from marriage there is no security for two people in a relationship. There may be a spoken promise; but if one person refuses to make the promise final through marriage, words are just words. Sex without that final promise will not build security. It will not hold someone responsible for his actions. That person is not accepted as the only person who is loved whatever happens. Instead he has value only for what he can do. It is against everything God wants in a relationship between two people.

Searching for Personal Closeness

Another reason young people hurry into sex is the attempt to find personal closeness in a relationship. Young people want to feel close to another person. They want to make an emotional connection and to feel especially loved.

The high level of sexual activity among young people shows how our culture is not able to experience true personal closeness. Emotional connection is the goal. Sex is often the means. Clearly, a physical act cannot help someone reach an emotional goal.

79

But for a young person seeking personal closeness, it can seem reasonable.

What is personal closeness? A 15-year-old girl once described personal closeness as a "place where it is safe to be real." A 16-year-old girl said that personal closeness is "being able to be real with another person." Most young people do not want sex as much as they want a close and caring relationship with another person. They just do not know how to find it.

The main problem in our culture is not sexual. It is relational. We have allowed our culture to tell us that the only way to find personal closeness is through touching another body.

Many people do not understand what real personal closeness is, so they are afraid of it. Why do people fear personal closeness? Because personal closeness is seen as weakness. Emotional sharing means telling about ourselves. For many of us the idea of opening up about ourselves is a fearful thing. Many young people share their bodies because they are afraid to share themselves. Like many older people, they mistake the excitement of sex for the personal closeness of love.

Real personal closeness is the result of letting another person see who you are. If you do not feel good about yourself, you will keep yourself hidden and never have personal closeness. Only a person with a good sense of security can fully enter into personal closeness.

True personal closeness means being able to remove all that we hide behind without fearing rejection. Then we can be known and loved for ourselves. The first step to that closeness is a life-changing relationship with Jesus Christ.

Searching for Friendship

The search for personal closeness is a search for friendship. People want to escape the loneliness that troubles our culture. Young people suffer the most from the pain of loneliness. Girls suffer more than boys do. That is another reason young people get involved in sex before marriage.

Sex before marriage is usually a search for a faithful relationship, not for sex. Yet sex can remove loneliness for a time. The fear of being lonely again makes young people keep having sex to keep that person. But what they are really looking for is love and friendship. A student wrote what I think is true for most young people today: "I want someone who cares. I want to love, and I want to be loved, but I do not know how to do either."

Unmarried young mothers who keep their babies usually do so to meet their own need for friendship. They want to have a child to love and to love them in return. One of the needs God created in people is the need for friendship. One of the first things God said about us was, "It is not good for man to be alone" (Genesis 2:18). Loneliness was not part of God's design for us.

When we admit that we are lonely and have a relational need, we are on the way to satisfying it. But a God-given desire can be met only in God's way.

Searching for an Escape from Fear of Rejection

When young people's lives are based on Christ, they are able to feel good about themselves. When the good feeling is based on a human relationship, young people may become dependent on that relationship. They feel good as long as the relationship is going well. They are afraid and feel rejected when things get hard.

If relationships are based on actions, the people being made to act are not in loving relationships. They can never feel at ease and secure. They can never be themselves. Young people in such a relationship need to get out of it immediately. Those who "give sex" out of fear of rejection are trying to buy security with their bodies.

Young people live in a world that demands immediate satisfaction. It is not surprising that they are filled with fear that by delaying sex until marriage they are being cheated. They are led to believe that sex is the best thing in life and that without it they may die a failure. So they have sex, but they come away empty. Then they have more sex to keep up with their friends. Without God and His Word, they do not know any better.

Another reason for sex before marriage is the fear of never finding a permanent friend in an always changing world. Fear is really a problem of inner peace. When people think that by changing their situation they will find happiness, they are fooling themselves. If they are not at peace in their present situation, they will not be at peace when change comes. The Bible says that complete peace is possible without marriage (read 1 Corinthians 7). Only God is able to provide peace in us. Marriage is not necessary. Neither is sex.

Searching for a Spiritual Connection

The Bible tells us that sex is a spiritual act as well as a physical act. That is probably why some people try to find spiritual oneness through sex. When two people are given to God and save sex until marriage, their sexual connection is a part of their spiritual connection. God is pleased and blesses them.

Oneness of spirit with another person can be good only if it is based on spiritual oneness with God. People who seek spiritual closeness with another person by disobeying biblical rules are destroying their relationship with God. God wants people to

82

draw near to each other spiritually. That is why we pray together, help each other in our walk with Christ and discuss spiritual concerns. These actions draw us closer to God.

Sex before marriage produces guilt and separates us from God. Sex can be a blessing only when it is part of God's plan, when it is an act of love within a marriage. Young people seeking for spiritual help in their lives through sex need to turn to God instead and be firmly rooted in Him.

Chapter 9

Everyone Is Doing It,
So Why Should We Wait?

One of the greatest pressures on young people today is the pressure to have sex. Young people are told that everyone is "doing it," and they do not want to be different. They think that if they just do what others are doing they will not feel so all alone.

The idea that everyone is doing it brings up two big questions. First, is it true that everyone is doing it? Second, are those who are doing it enjoying it? A study by *Seventeen* magazine tried to answer those two questions. The people who did the study talked with five hundred males and five hundred females between the ages of 13 and 21.

Seventy-three percent of the girls in the study said they would have sex only if their boyfriends pressured them. Sixty-seven percent of the girls said they were already sexually active. Eighty-one percent of the girls who were sexually active said they were sorry they had done it.[1]

Some young people are made to believe that they are the last young person in the country who has not had sex. But that is not true. From 20 percent to 35 percent of young people have never had sex. For Christian young people the numbers are from 30 percent to 45 percent.

We can learn four things from these numbers. First, our culture is experiencing an almost complete change in values. Second, many Christian young people are following culture instead of obeying God's commands. Third, Christian young people who are not going along with the culture are not being left out. They are the ones holding out against the culture. And fourth, up to 35 percent of young people are not following the culture. For Christian young people that is as high as 45 percent.

Young people who think that everyone is doing it are looking in the wrong places. They should be looking at older brothers or sisters who may not be doing it. They should be looking for other young people their age who are not doing it. Church is the best place to look.

Many of the young people who are having sex are not enjoying it as much as we are led to believe. For some girls sex is a painful thing. They go through it only to please a boy they like. They do not enjoy it while it is happening, and their consciences hurt them later. They do not feel good about themselves. The pain often is greater than the gain.

Young people who are not sexually active and feel left out should think of themselves in a new way. Instead of feeling out of step with the culture, they should understand that the culture is out of step with God. Here are some of the ways young people are answering the claim that everyone is doing it:

I am not everyone. I am me. Besides, I do not really believe everyone is doing it. I think that is just talk.

* * * * *

If everyone is doing it, then you should not have too much trouble finding another person to do it with.

* * * * *

Yes, I can see that more and more girls are getting pregnant.

* * * * *

"Everyone is doing it" is a very poor reason to do anything. That pressure does not affect me because I do not want what "everyone" has. I do not want sexually transmitted diseases, divorce or a broken home. I do not want to get pregnant before I get married.

* * * * *

How often something happens does not show its value. For example, let us say that most people get cancer. Does that mean that I should want to get cancer?

But let us be honest. Not many young people are brave enough to give any of these answers to the pressure to have sex. They are looking for ways to fit in and be accepted. They do not want to be different.

Our world says, "If it feels good, do it!" In God's kingdom, though, the command is, "Be holy, for I the Lord your God am holy" (Leviticus 19:2). We must choose which way we will take.

Pressure to Be Like Others

Young people write to me about the pressure to be good enough.

Our parents and our teachers make us feel that we are not good enough if we do not get good grades in school. Our friends put the same kind of pressure on us to have sex.

* * * * *

The pressure from our friends is the greatest. They call us cowards. They laugh at our fear of getting pregnant.

* * * * *

The most important thing in life is what our best friends think about us.

Young people want to wear the same kind of shoes their friends wear. They want to have their hair cut in the same way and wear the same kinds of clothes. They want to watch the same television shows and go to the same movies. They want to be just like their friends. When their friends are having sex, they feel the pressure to have sex also.

Young people today spend most of their time with other young people. That is true even in church. That means that the greatest influences in their lives are other young people and the popular culture. When those influences say to have sex, it is hard for the young person to refuse.

Young people who are trying to fit in with the world need to see themselves as God sees them. They need to understand that their worth as a person is not based on their willingness to have sex. They need to understand that they are special in God's sight. Then they will be able to treat others as special also.

Pressure from a Boyfriend or a Girlfriend

Probably the greatest pressure young people face about sex is the pressure from a boyfriend or a girlfriend. In one study more than half of the young people who had had sex said that they first did so with a steady boyfriend or girlfriend.[2] ("Steady" means that a boy promises not to date any other girls and the girl promises not to date any other boys.) Girls feel that pressure more than boys do. They may feel that they "owe" it to the boy. Or they may be afraid the boy will leave them if they do not do what he wants.

Here are parts of some letters girls have sent me:

> I was afraid, but I wanted to please him so that I would not lose him. The first time was the biggest mistake of my life. After that, desire for love became so strong that I could not oppose it.

* * * * *

Some of my friends have sex because they are afraid of losing their boyfriend or that a boy will not ask them out for a second date. Some of them will go against what they think is right if they think the relationship is in danger.

* * * * *

Deciding not to have sex can mean the end of a relationship. But usually it means that the relationship would not have continued much longer anyway.

And here are some ways girls have responded to the pressure from their boyfriends:

I just explain that I am not ready for sex yet. I say something like, "It is easy for you to never call or speak to me again, but I have to live with myself in the morning."

* * * * *

If that is the way you feel, I will miss seeing you. But that is the way it has to be.

* * * * *

If all I mean to you is a body to have sex with, maybe we should take a closer look at why we see each other. You have no right to use me.

True love wants to give and help. It honors the other person and makes her feel good about herself. True love thinks about the results of an action. It always acts in the other person's best interest.

Too often young people use sex as a way to escape from problems. But having sex brings on a whole new set of problems. Instead of having sex, the young person should deal with his problem in an effective way. The first step in dealing with a problem is to admit that a problem exists and that it is having a bad effect. Then the young person should try to understand why the problem exists. Finally he needs to seek help from someone who is able to show him how to deal with the problem.

God has given Christian young people three helpers for dealing with problems. The Bible, the Holy Spirit, and loving relationships within the family and the church.

The Pressure of Sex Education in School

A boy in his first year of high school gave me this report:

> The school nurse was teaching a sex education class. One day she was telling us all the ways to keep from getting pregnant. She finished by saying, "The only way that is 100 percent sure is to not have sex, but we cannot expect young people to wait until marriage."

That is the opinion of our culture, that we cannot expect young people to wait until marriage to have sex. That is why sex education must begin in the home. Parents and churches must give their young people good reasons to wait.

In the past six chapters we have been examining six main reasons why young people do not wait until marriage to have sex. In the next six chapters we will discuss some of the most important reasons why they should wait.

Chapter 10
God's Protection and Provision

Dana is 18 years old. This is her first year living away from home to attend school. She keeps very busy and still gets very good grades. This has been a very exciting year for her, especially because she has a very nice-looking boyfriend, Troy. They have been dating for eight months and getting to know each other really well. They have not had sex yet, but both of them are feeling the desire to do so. She is feeling the pressure from every side to do it.

When Troy asked Dana to go away with him for a few days, she knew exactly what he meant. She knew that her parents did not approve of sex before marriage. She had never before thought about going against their wishes. But she is beginning to wonder now. All her friends tell her to do it. Her best friend says, "As long as you are planning to get married, there is no reason to wait to have sex." All the media agree, "It is your body, so you are free to choose. Do what feels right for you."

With all these voices pulling her one way, Dana is not sure what to do. There is one voice she has not yet considered, though. She has not yet considered what God has to say about it. If I remind her of that, though, she might say, "Now you are talking about rules. I am talking about love."

I would tell Dana that I am also talking about love. I am not talking about Troy's love for her but about God's love for her. The God who created the worlds also created Dana. Long ago David wrote, "You made the parts inside me. You put me together inside my mother" (Psalm 139:13). He said, "O Lord, You have looked through me and have known me. You know when I sit down and when I get up. You understand my thoughts from far away" (Psalm 139:1-2).

Not only did God make us, but He loves us. "For God so loved the world that He gave His only Son. Whoever puts his trust in God's Son will not be lost but will have life that lasts forever" (John 3:16). Whenever God tells us what to do, He does it because He loves us.

Dana might say, "I do not believe God loves me. If He did why would He say 'do not' so many times in the Bible? He only wants to keep me from having fun. That is not love." That is just the way many young people feel about God. Let me tell you how I answer that argument.

God Proves His Love by Saying "No"

Think about the life of Christ as it is given in the gospels of Matthew, Mark, Luke and John. He went about doing good. He provided the drink for a wedding party (John 2:1-11). Two times He fed great crowds of people when they were hungry (Matthew 14:13-21; 15:29-39). He gave sight to the blind and hearing to the deaf. He healed all kinds of diseases. He even raised several dead people. He was known as the Friend of sinners (Luke 7:34). He never did anything to hurt anyone.

Never forget that God always deals with us out of a heart of love. He does not just say He loves us. He shows His love in many ways. We may not believe Him, but we can give no good reason why we should not believe Him.

Parents show their love for their small children by saying, "Do not play in the street." The foolish child may think that the parents are keeping him from having fun. But what is so fun about being hit by a truck? The wise child will trust his parents and obey even if he does not understand. Someday he will understand the need for such a rule. Then he will certainly agree that it was best to obey his parents. He may even thank them that they loved him enough to make such a rule.

In the same way God shows His love by telling us to not do the things He knows will hurt us. If we are wise, we will obey Him even if we do not understand. We will obey even if everyone around us is not obeying. We will obey God because we know He loves us and has our best interests at heart.

Here is what one young person wrote to me:

> People often feel that God's commands are there to keep them back from having a good time. We need to listen to how Christ answered His own question. "What man among you would give his son a stone if he should ask for bread? Or if he asks for a fish, would he give him a snake? You are bad and you know how to give good things to your children. How much more will your Father in heaven give good things to those who ask Him?" (Matthew 7:9-11).

God's Rules Protect Us and Provide for Us

Thinking that God's rules keep us from having fun is like a fish in a glass bowl. The owner of the fish feeds it and changes the water often to keep it clean and fresh. He sets the bowl in a safe place so that the cat cannot get the fish. He puts the bowl where it will be warm in the cold part of the year and cool in the hot part of the year. Everything the fish could possibly want is right there in that bowl.

Imagine, though, that the fish looked at the world outside his bowl and decided that he wanted to be out there. Day after day he thinks only of gaining his freedom. He dreams of the exciting things he could do if only he were not held prisoner in the bowl. Finally one day he makes the jump. He is out of the bowl and onto the floor. But instead of enjoying his freedom he is soon dead.

The fish would have done much better to have remained within the limits set for him by a wise owner. God is our owner. We do well to be satisfied to remain within the limits He sets for us. His rules are there to protect us and to provide for us. They keep us from harm and meet our every need.

God made the world and us. He made sex for our enjoyment. But because He knows that sex used in the wrong way can lead to great harm, He gave us rules to guide our actions. As long as we obey those rules, we are safe and can enjoy sex to its fullest. If we disobey God's rules about sex, we must suffer the results.

There is only one main rule about sex: do not have sex outside of marriage. The other rules about sex only show us how to put that one rule to work in our lives.

Chapter 11
The Physical Reasons to Wait

People who have sex before marriage cannot really be free in their enjoyment of sex. That is because they cannot escape the physical results. Those results are of two kinds. One kind is sexually transmitted diseases (STDs). The other kind of result is the difficulties that can come from an unwanted pregnancy. Young people who wait until marriage have God's protection from both. They also enjoy the blessing of a guilt-free relationship in their marriage in the future.

In God's perfect plan for sex, everything is good and enjoyable. Sex ties a husband and wife together in a way that no other thing can. That is why God tells us to wait until marriage. He does not want us to ruin a good thing.

Sex within marriage is within God's design, and so it is good. Sex outside of marriage is outside of God's design, and so it cannot really be good. It may feel good at the time, but it is never a truly good thing.

One study shows that the people who are best satisfied with their present sex life are married people.[1] They strongly believe that sex outside of marriage is wrong. That is just one evidence of God's provision and protection within marriage.

Sexually Transmitted Diseases

Young people should wait for sex until marriage. Many young people who do not wait get an STD. That may be because they do not understand the danger of having sex outside of a permanent marriage relationship. One study showed that girls were not influenced even when they knew about STDs.[2] They knew the facts, but they did not understand the dangers.

A person can be carrying one or more STDs and not even know it. If another person has sex with that person, he could catch as many as five different STDs in just one time of having sex.[3] A few years ago there were only five kinds of STDs. Now there are more than twenty-seven kinds.

A few years ago a person who had sex outside of marriage did not have to be much concerned about STDs. Not many people had an STD. That has changed as more and more people are having sex with more people who are not a life-time husband or wife. Now millions of people every year catch an STD. When two people have sex, they are really having sex with all the people the other person has ever had sex with. That explains why STDs are spreading so rapidly.

A woman with an STD who gets pregnant is more likely to have the baby born before it is ready. When the baby is born, it is more likely to have serious health problems.

Sex outside of marriage is more than just a small problem. STDs can kill! The most dangerous STD is AIDS. Of the 513,486 people in the United States who were known to have AIDS through December 1995, more than 62 percent (319,849) died by 2002. That is, three out of five people with AIDS died in just seven years.

Other kinds of STDs can cause some kinds of cancer. That also can lead to death.

HIV/AIDS

HIV is a condition that weakens the body so that it cannot fight off disease. Many people who have HIV will get AIDS. A person with AIDS will feel tired and have an increased body temperature. He loses interest in eating and so loses weight. His head may hurt, and he may often want to sleep when he should be awake. He will grow weak and will often feel sick. In the end he will die from a disease he gets because he has AIDS. There is no cure. However, new medical treatment can help a person with AIDS live longer than was the case several years ago.

Most people who get HIV do so in one of three ways. They may get it through using illegal drugs. They may get it through receiving blood from someone who has HIV. Or they may get HIV by having sex with a person who has HIV.

In 1996 the World Health Organization reported:

> There are more than 3 million new cases of AIDS. Most of these people were under the age of 25. . . . The new cases bring to nearly 23 million the number of people who have AIDS. In the fifteen years since AIDS was discovered, 6.4 million people have died from the disease. One million of these were children. . . . Of the 8,500 new cases each day, 1,000 are children. About 42 percent of all those living with HIV are women, and that percentage is growing.[4]

A later World Health Organization report showed:

- In 1999 there were 5.4 million new cases of HIV.

- There were 34.3 million people living with HIV/ AIDS.

- In 1999 2.8 million people died of AIDS.

- From 1981 to 1999 there were 18.8 million deaths from AIDS.

God's protection from this deadly disease is one good reason for young people to say no to sex before marriage. Here are some other important things you should know about HIV/AIDS:

- AIDS is the leading cause of death for Americans between the ages of 25 and 44.[5] Many of these get HIV before they are 20 years old.[6]

- Four of ten people with HIV do not tell the person they want to have sex with that they have HIV.[7]

- People who have another STD have a greater chance of getting HIV.[8]

- Babies born to women with HIV have a great chance of having HIV when they are born.[9]

- Every year thousands of new mothers with HIV/AIDS die when their babies are born.

One of the fastest growing AIDS groups in America is young people. Most of these are boys who are having sex with other boys. But many girls also have HIV/AIDS.[10]

Chlamydia

Chlamydia is another new STD. It was first reported in the United States in 1995. By 1998 there were 1,665 new cases reported every day. Five percent of sexually active young people get chlamydia every year. Girls between the ages of 16 and 19 have the highest rate of getting chlamydia.

Chlamydia has become one of the most common STDs in America, and one of the most dangerous. It is most common among young people before the age of 20. At least 10 percent of sexually active young people have chlamydia. They may have it for years without knowing they have it.

Eighty percent of the girls and 40 percent of the boys who have chlamydia do not know they have it.[11] Even though they do not know they have chlamydia, they can still pass it on to others through having sex. Because so many have chlamydia without knowing it, it is not possible to know how many young people have it.

When a person has chlamydia, she may not be able to have children. That may sound like a blessing for unmarried people. But when they get married and want to start a family, it will not be good news. And even if a woman does become pregnant, the child may die or be born with serious health problems. Sometimes the mother also dies when the baby is born.

There is a drug that can cure chlamydia, but a person can get the disease again.[12] In fact, 40 percent of the girls who have been cured get the disease again within 14 months.[13] Each time a woman has chlamydia she has an increased chance of not being able to have children in the future.

As with other STDs, no young person has to get chlamydia. There are two steps to protect yourself from chlamydia. First, wait until marriage to have sex. Second, both husband and wife remain faithful to each other in marriage.

PID

In girls, chlamydia can result in a condition known as PID. PID can also result from having gonorrhea. We will talk about gonorrhea next. Fifteen-year-old girls have a far greater chance of getting PID than do older women under the same conditions. A girl of 15 has a 12 percent chance of getting PID when she has sex. A woman of 24 has less than a 2 percent chance.[14]

A girl with PID will experience pain that does not go away until she is treated by a doctor for the disease. Some cases of PID can be cured with drugs. Harder cases can be treated only through surgery. The surgery leaves the girl unable to have children. Even without surgery, though, she may never be able to have children. One in seven women who ever has PID will never be able to have children.[15] If a woman has PID three times, there is a 75 percent chance she will never be able to become pregnant.[16]

If a girl who has had PID does become pregnant, it may be difficult for her to give birth. That may cause the death of the baby. Sometimes it causes the death of the mother.

Girls who wait until marriage to have sex are protected from PID.

Gonorrhea

Gonorrhea is one of the most common STDs. It is also one of the oldest. It has been around for at least twenty-five hundred years. Now it is so common all over the world that there are 250 million new cases every year. In the United States alone there are 750,000 new cases reported every year. But because many cases are never reported, there may be as many as 3 million new cases each year.

The only way to get gonorrhea is to have sex with a person who has it. But as many as 80 percent of women who have gonorrhea do not have any signs of the disease.[17] That means that they can pass it along to others without even knowing that they are doing so. When a boy has sex with a girl who has gonorrhea, there is a 30 percent chance that he will get it. But when a girl has sex with a boy who has gonorrhea, there is a 90 percent chance she will get it.[18]

As with PID, girls 15 to 19 years of age have a greater chance of getting gonorrhea than do older women.[19] Many young people believe that using a condom protects them from getting gonorrhea, but that is only partly true. Many times the condom fails to protect.

By itself gonorrhea is not as harmful as many other STDs. The problem is that gonorrhea opens the door to some of the most harmful ones. That is, a person with gonorrhea is more likely to get HIV or herpes.[20]

However, gonorrhea does have some harmful effects. Pain, especially back pain, is common. Many girls who have gonorrhea even one time will never be able to have children. And if a person has gonorrhea one time there is an increased chance that he will have it again. That only increases the chance that a girl will never be able to have children. If she does have a child later, the child may be born blind.

Genital Herpes (HSV)

This disease almost always comes from having sex. A mother can also pass it on to her new baby.[21] From 50 to 90 percent of people with this disease do not know they have it. A doctor can tell only through using tests. There is no medical cure for HSV. People who have it may sometimes seem to be free of it only to have it return later. Condoms do very little to stop the spread of HSV.[22]

About 45 million people in the United States have this disease. That means one out of six Americans has it. Women with HSV are eight times as likely to develop cancer as those who do not have the disease.[23] HSV is a little more common in women than in men.

Think about it: about one in every six people you see every day has HSV. Most of them do not even know it, so they continue to give it to others by having sex with them. For most people who have HSV, the disease will come and go several times a year. The times become less often over the years. After eight years, the HSV will usually come just three times a year.

A study reported that 46 percent of all African-Americans over the age of 11 show evidence of having HSV.[24]

New babies may suffer from their mothers' HSV. Even with the right treatment, up to 54 percent of the babies will die. Those who live may have problems for a long time. Their minds may not work as well, and they may have problems learning. They also may go blind.[25]

A teacher from George Washington University reports "very bad guilt feelings" among women who get the disease. Many of the women say they feel unclean and dirty. The only way to be completely safe from HSV is to have no sex before marriage. Marry a person who has had no sex before marriage. Remain with the same husband or wife for life.

Genital Warts from Human Papillomavirus (HPV)

As with many STDs, most people with HPV do not know they have the disease. Sometimes only a doctor can tell if a wart is a genital wart. Genital warts are the most common STD, but they can be treated and cured. A difficulty may come in the early stages of the disease, however, and there is no help for it. The National Institute of Health says, "Condoms provide almost no protection against HPV."[26]

Perhaps the most surprising fact is that 80 million Americans between 15 and 49 years of age have had genital HPV at some point in their lives!

HPV may be caught very easily. Up to 90 percent of people who have sex with someone who has HPV get it. The following studies are bad enough. But many who have this disease never report it because of shame or because they do not know they have it.

- Only 2 percent of men or women who have HPV show any signs that they have it.[27]
- HPV will kill 5,000 women in the United States this year and 245,000 more in the rest of the world.[28]

101

- Doctors have found 80 kinds of HPV.[29]
- HPV is the cause of most cancer of the reproductive organs of both men and women.
- If you do not already have HPV, the only way for you to keep from getting it is to establish a permanent one husband-one wife relationship before you have sex again. That is called "marriage."[30]

Syphilis

Syphilis is a disease that comes mainly through having sex. About half of all people who have syphilis do not know they have it. This is either because their bodies do not show it or because they believe the painless marks on their skin are harmless. Syphilis has been a health problem in the United States for many years.

With the coming of penicillin, the number of new cases of syphilis went down. That caused two things to happen. First, health-care officials reduced their attempts to control syphilis. Second, sex outside of marriage in the United States increased. By the early 1990s, reported cases were at their highest level in 40 years. That number has since gone down again, but syphilis is still the eighth most commonly reported spreadable disease in the United States.[31]

Trichomoniasis

There are about 5 million new cases of trichomoniasis each year in the United States.[32] It can come along with several other STDs. It may cause cancer.[33]

Hepatitus B

There is no known cure for hepatitus B. It is believed that in the United States alone at least 100,000 people get this disease each year as a result of having sex. Hepatitis B is 10 times more easily caught than HIV.[34] It is present in about 60 to 70 percent of all men who have sex with other men.[35] In 1995 doctors wrote about their concern for unborn babies having the disease at birth.[36]

Cancer

Cancer is one of the most feared diseases that comes from sex outside of marriage. In 1999 a new examination of the facts found in earlier studies showed that HPV disease was really present in almost all cases of cervical cancer.[37] The earlier a girl begins having sex, the higher her possibility of developing cervical cancer as a woman. Hepatitis B can cause liver cancer, one of the most common cancers. Other STDs can cause other cancers.

Unwanted Pregnancy

Another reason young people must say no to sex before marriage is the possibility of an unwanted pregnancy. That will make them parents before they are ready for the responsibility. Here is one student's thoughts on this:

> There is no 100 percent protection. Pregnancy is always a possibility. Many young people think they will not get caught. They use that as an excuse for having sex. They think, "God will not allow me to get pregnant and ruin my life." They think He is in the business of helping us sin. There is a price to pay for sin. Even David was caught, and he was a man after God's own heart. The Bible gives the results of his actions: David's son died and his family was shamed .

If our culture will not explain the bad effects of sex before marriage, the church must be willing to speak up. Young people must be taught what God says about sex. They must learn why He gives commands about sex and how He provides for and protects those who obey. Young people must know what might happen if they do not obey.

A pregnant girl has one of four roads open to her. First, she can give her baby up for adoption. Second, she can marry the father of the child. Third, she can raise the child alone. Fourth, she can have the baby killed before it is born. Whatever she decides, she probably will have to make that decision alone. Most of the men who get young girls pregnant will leave them. She may not even be able to turn to her family.

The health problems for young mothers and their babies are huge. Many pregnant young women do not take care of their health and that can make problems for the babies born to them. As the values in our country continue to change, young people will continue to pay a high price for unwanted pregnancies.

Abortion

If being a parent or giving the child up for adoption is not chosen, many girls consider abortion. Abortion is killing the baby before it is born. In the United States an abortion takes place every 22 seconds. Here is what one student wrote me:

> Abortion is also called a "way out." But do two wrongs make a right? Should murder be added to adultery to make everything right? Many women who have abortions are later unable to have children. That danger alone should be enough to make them save sex for marriage.

Abortion may seem like the easy way out from an unwanted pregnancy, but the damage to the mother is often not considered. Recent studies have shown a possible link between abortions and breast cancer. That alone destroys the idea of sex before marriage being "safe." Doctors who do abortions are being urged to tell those who seek an abortion everything that is known about abortion.[38]

Those who accept the idea of abortion talk about the woman's rights over her own body. But what about the rights of the unborn baby? Some British experts say that "unborn babies feel pain as early as 26 weeks."

The young mother, too, often suffers great damage to her emotions. That damage may trouble her for many years.

The world does not give the right answers to the problems of young people's pregnancies. The answer is to take God at His Word and understand that His wise commands are there for our own good. He has provided sex so that married people can have children and raise them in the ways of the Lord. The book of Proverbs says children are a blessing. In a loving marriage, that is just what they are. As the father of four children, I know that is true.

God's commands are given for our protection. He does not want anyone ever to have to decide about an unwanted pregnancy. So He tells us to wait to have sex until marriage. His way is so simple. It seems to be too simple for the modern mind.

Chapter 12
The Emotional Reasons to Wait

Young people should wait until marriage to have sex to escape the emotional pain that comes from sex before marriage. They should accept God's protection from emotional problems and His provision for a rich, guilt-free marriage.

There is no way to measure the damaging effect of sex before marriage. But getting involved in sex before trust and security have been developed can hurt a future permanent relationship.

Protection from the Emotional Traps of Sex Before Marriage

The terrible emotional results that sex before marriage can bring may be immediate, or they may be delayed for a time. Some people may be able to work through their problems by prayer and the help of friends. But the problems may last for years. Here are some of the problems God will protect young people from if they remain sexually pure.

Protection from Guilt

Guilt is one result of sex before marriage. Guilt may trouble a person longer than any other result. It can keep a person from spiritual growth and emotional well-being. The Bible says, "Marriage should be respected by everyone. God will punish those who do sex sins and are not faithful in marriage" (Hebrews 13:4). Even those who do not know God's laws may feel guilty because they are guilty before a holy God.

Guilt is knowing one has disobeyed a rule of right and wrong. Or it is the feeling that perhaps an act was wrong. This second kind of guilt can be called a floating sense of guilt. It comes from saying there is no right and wrong. People who say that have no order in their lives. They have no rules by which to measure actions. They live with a sense of guilt, but they do not understand the reasons for their guilt.

Christians have the Bible. It shows the nature of God and His plan for man. It shows how we can have a relationship with Him. It also gives us the only way of deciding what is right and what is wrong. By accepting God's way, Christians have order in their lives.

God has put limits around us to keep us safe. Inside those limits we have freedom to choose. Persons outside of God's limits live without direction and feel lost. For example, God has provided marriage as the place for sex. Persons living within God's limits are free to marry or not marry. If they decide to marry, they are able to enjoy closeness in a situation where no one can be hurt.

Protection from Being Judged About How Well You Do Sex

Sexually active people are concerned only with how well the other person can please them. When people are accepted only by how well they can please another person sexually, the value given to them by God is lost. Without the promise given in marriage, sex is only for selfish enjoyment. The people have no security in their relationship. They have an unspoken fear of being rejected.

One husband and wife were having sexual problems. After getting advice, the husband learned that his wife had been mistreated sexually as a child. Wanting to help her, he bought the book *The Joy of Sex*. His wife went back to the one who had been advising them and said, "I know he is trying to help me. But this book just makes me feel worse. All it deals with is body positions and things two bodies can do to each other. After I looked through it, I felt like a piece of meat, something to be used to please another person."

Most books about sex deal with it only on a physical level. That can make a person feel that only actions count. Both husband and wife need to know that they are free to make mistakes. They need to be on firm ground emotionally and spiritually so that the expression of their love can be free.

Protection from Wrong Ideas About Sex and Love

One of the reasons I hear given most often for sexual involvement is mistaking sex for love. This shows in what one girl wrote:

> I remember when the "love" I had been waiting for came along. Three months after we started dating, we began having sex. Then we stayed away from other people as much as possible in order to be alone together. But we really only wanted to satisfy our physical hunger. We really thought of this as love!

When we mistake sex for love, we have not understood the simple idea of giving and taking. Love always gives. Sex before marriage takes. The problem is, the taking can sometimes look like giving. A girl may "give her boyfriend what he wants," making it look as if she is giving him love. Really she wants the security he provides. Her "giving" is really a form of taking.

Sex before marriage can lead a person to marry the wrong person. Sex can create a strong tie, making the young people believe the relationship is more than it really is. By telling us to keep sex for marriage, God protects us from the terrible effects that such emotions can have.

Our goal as Christians is to grow in godly love. That is the kind of love that gives without expecting anything in return.

In 1 Corinthians 13 love is described as acts of the will. Yet love has great emotional force because it has to do with how we connect with people. God meant for sex to be a joining of the heart and the soul of two people. That is why sex before marriage can leave us feeling good for a short time but after that bad emotions set in. When we deal with right and wrong things, we are faced with right and wrong results.

Protection from Becoming a Slave to Sex

Once young people have experienced the excitement of sex, the desire for sex grows. Here is how one student described the desire:

> The more sexually involved I became, the more I wished for this 'great experience.' Looking back on that part of my life, I think I was a slave to sex. I never found a balance. I never found real love. The more I searched for love, the more unhappy I became.

Books on science often say that man is an animal. They say that our desire for sex is the same as what other animals experience. Sex is seen as a need. Such thinking robs a person of self-worth and the value of life.

God created us to be like Him. We have needs for food, water and housing; but our greatest need is to know God. In order to establish that relationship, we have to admit our failings and confess our need for God. Some people refuse to do that. Instead of having their greatest need met by knowing God, they look for other ways to fill it. Once they say sex is a need, they allow themselves the freedom to have sex as often as they wish. As a result they fail time after time because they are trying to fill a spiritual need with physical enjoyment.

Sexual desire drives many young people apart. One student wrote:

> Although having sex does hurt a relationship, it also makes it harder for two people to end the relationship. Separating after you have had sex together can be a terrible experience emotionally. Sex creates an emotional tie so powerful it must be kept for marriage.

It is impossible for two people to have sex without getting involved at a level deeper than the body. That is just the way God made us. Sex connects people emotionally and spiritually as well as physically.

Sex forms an emotional tie that can remain even when the relationship goes bad. The longer the sexual activity continues, the harder it is to stop. But for the problems in the relationship to be solved, the unmarried people must separate. They are better off spiritually and emotionally. They are better off mentally and possibly even physically.

One girl wrote about how she had slept with a boy for four years. Then they had an argument. The thought of separating hurt so much that she turned to God. But she still did not have enough faith to say no to sex. She said her boyfriend was a Christian, too. But he saw nothing wrong in having sex as long as they loved each other. She wondered how they could fight this sexual desire. They had talked about it many times but talking never helped.

The answer for this girl is not "more faith." The answer is for her to separate from her boyfriend. The pull of sex is very hard to stop when it has been a part of a relationship for a long time. That is true even if they both agree it is wrong. It is even harder if one says it is wrong while the other says it is not wrong.

Another common emotional effect of sex before marriage is bitterness. One feels bitter toward the other because of the sexual acts that have happened.

Protection from a Poor Idea of Self-worth

How we decide things is greatly influenced by the way we think about ourselves. People who see themselves as God sees them have a good feeling of self-worth. They do not need to depend on another person to feel good about themselves.

People with poor self-worth will seek help from another person in order to feel good about themselves. Sex is a common tool used in that situation. This sad note shows how it goes:

> I think my heart became more hard. After a while, I did not care if I loved the boy. I did not like doing it that much, and I did not even care who I did it with. My self-worth went way down. I stopped caring anything about myself.

Sex, as it should be in marriage, is based on security. In God's plan for sex, there is complete love and trust. God designed marriage to be a permanent relationship in which the people have complete security. But people think their plans are better.

Young people expect too much from sex. They think sex can work wonders, making them see themselves better and making them look better in another person's eyes. One of the greatest things they expect is to establish a closeness. They hope that through physical closeness they can find emotional closeness and so feel better about themselves.

When God commands us to save sex for marriage, He does it to protect us. Young people need to grow nearer to God in a personal relationship with Jesus Christ. Then they will understand that they do not need the temporary acceptance of others to have a healthy self-worth. They will understand that they are complete in Christ and are accepted by God just as they are. Then they will be free to give to others and do not have to take from them.

Provision for Emotional Wholeness in a Future Marriage

God wants to provide for young people the emotional and mental wholeness that results from saving sex for marriage. One young person said it well: "I choose to invest in loving, caring relationships that do not include sex. These relationships include the kind of emotional help, satisfaction and direction that keep me going in life. Sex alone cannot do that."

Provision of Maturity

One of the marks of being mature, or being an adult, is to be able to delay satisfaction. We live in a do-it-now world. In other words, our world is not mature; and it urges young people to live in an immature way.

Life is a plan, and developing into an adult is part of that plan. It does not happen immediately. God provides for us by having us wait until marriage to have sex. He builds goodness and maturity in our lives as we show self-control and obey Him. Physical satisfaction does not last long. Maturity can never be taken away.

Provision of True Love

Waiting for sex until marriage allows true love to develop in a relationship. Love always seeks the best interest of the one loved. That is why we can have security in God's love. He will never do or say anything that is not in our best interest. God tells us to wait until marriage for sex to provide a solid base for our relationship in marriage.

First Corinthians 13 always comes up when Christians talk about love. This Scripture gives us rules by which we can measure our actions and feelings. Think again about these words:

> Love does not give up. Love is kind. Love is not jealous. Love does not put itself up as being important. Love has no pride. Love does not do the wrong thing. Love never thinks of itself. Love does not get angry. Love does not remember the suffering that comes from being hurt by someone. Love is not happy with sin. Love is happy with the truth. Love takes everything that comes without giving up. Love believes all things. Love hopes for all things. Love keeps on in all things. (1 Corinthians 13:4-7)

If you think you are in love, put your name in the place of the word "love." Then read the Scripture again putting the name of the other person in the place of the word "love." If you are in a sex-before-marriage relationship, this list will not fit you very well.

Provision of Value of One's Body

Our bodies are described in the Bible as houses where the Holy Spirit lives (1 Corinthians 6:19-20). One of God's provisions for those who save sex for marriage is a healthy value of their bodies, God's house. One student said:

> Your body is something you should save for your husband or wife, not some one-night experiment. If you think you have found the one you really love and he says he loves you, he will wait. Do not fall for the old line, "If you love me, you will do it." If he tries that, just say, "If you love me, you will wait."

Provision of Honor

We are valuable because God made us like Himself. God does not just show us His love. He is love. When we understand that, we will accept everything about ourselves as gifts from God. Those of us who have accepted His forgiveness and given our lives to Him have an added measure of honor. We are workers with Him. We are called to live worthy of our high calling.

Human sexuality is a part of the honor God has given to us. In the right time and the right place, it can be expressed in sex. When we have sex before we should, though, we hurt ourselves and the calling we have been given.

Provision for Only One "First Time"

After hearing me speak at a "Why True Love Waits" meeting, a 17-year-old girl wrote to me:

> You helped me when you told why God wants us to wait and told of the beauty He means sex to be. So Tuesday I had lunch with friends who have always made fun of me for not having sex. I said, "I do not want any more jokes about my not having sex because any day I can become like you, but you can never again become like me."

Many people have thanked me for helping them cool their relationship for a while in order to stop the sexual action that was making slaves of them. Almost all who went on to get married were thankful for that waiting period.

Provision for Closeness

True closeness between a man and a woman is another one of God's provisions for young people who say no to sex before marriage. To be able to be open with someone, we must first have security in ourselves. Then we must have a sense of security in the relationship that tells us our openness will not be hurt. That security can be found only in God.

Closeness is built by trust. It has two parts. First, by faith we must know our position in Jesus Christ. When we know we are important to God, we have security and can develop a healthy sense of self-worth.

Second, we must feel loved and accepted by some other person in our lives. In this way we see God expressing His love for us. We must see that it is possible for someone to accept us whatever we do. Then we can be loving and accepting toward others. We must learn to love. This is God's plan.

Chapter 13

Reasons to Wait Because of Relationships

Young people often do not have enough experience of life to become parents. Neither do they have the lifetime promise of faithfulness that comes with marriage. That is why sex can do more harm than good for their relationships. God wants young people to enjoy closeness in relationships both now and when they marry. But He has kept physical closeness for marriage. Let us see how sex before marriage separates young people from God's protection and provision in their relationships.

Protection from Unhealthy Relationships

God wants to protect young people from pain in their relationships with other people. That is why He says no to sex before marriage.

Protection from a Social Crash

We all want to love and be loved. We all want to connect with other people at a deep level. Sex before marriage will cut short that relationship. When young people delay sex until marriage, they allow the relationship to grow and become strong. Then sex can have meaning and be good for the relationship. Until marriage, the young man and young woman need to spend time learning about each other. They can see what makes the other person unusual and desirable. This lays the base for love and leads to the personal closeness each one seeks.

Getting into sex before marriage may make it impossible to ever make a relationship right. Here is what one student discovered: "Another situation to consider – social connection. You are getting to know and enjoy a person. You like it when he allows you to see him as he really is. But when sex starts, the lines of social connection break down."

Protection from Difficult Times Before Marriage

One of the gifts God allows us to give another person is showing self-control. When we establish a relationship, self-control must be present for trust to be built. Trust is the base for any continued growth in the relationship. Sex before marriage hurts such trust by showing that a person is not in control of his desires. Instead, he is controlled by his desires. That makes the relationship suffer and may end it.

The longer a relationship continues, the more pain there is when it is ended. That is why God commands us, "Have nothing to do with sex sins!" When sex is not a part of the relationship, people are better able to understand each other. They can know for certain if they are choosing the right person to marry. By obeying God's commands about sex before marriage, we are under God's protection and able to receive His provision.

Protection from Comparison

Why does it trouble people so much when they remember past sexual experiences? God created the sexual experience to give us the best memories we will ever have. There are two main ways to understand human memory: (1) the study of the brain and (2) the study of the way memory works and the things we remember. We will look at the second way because it is more helpful for our purpose.

Science has discovered a number of elements that help us understand why memories about sex are so strong and permanent. One element is how memories become memories that we keep for a long time. There are at least two important facts involved in creating a memory that lasts: (1) the greatness of the experience and (2) how much we go over the experience in our minds. Sex is likely to be involved in both of these.

Another element of memory is that people remember more clearly when the emotions are involved. The more of our five senses involved in an experience, the more likely we are to remember. Our five senses are sight, touch, hearing, taste and smell. These senses can all be involved in sex. Something from within us (thoughts, feelings, actions) or from without (through our five senses) reminds us of something similar from our past.

A young person who has had sex before marriage probably will not have the same feelings when he has sex later. This is especially true if the earlier times involved hurt, mistrust or guilt. When past experiences are brought into marriage, there is trouble.

We can see that the most important part of sex is our mind. Really that is good news! Think of what happens when two people learn about sex from their first time together within marriage. Good memories are formed that tie those two people together in a loving, trusting way without any problems from the past.

God has given us His commands to wait for sex until marriage to protect us from unfair comparisons. When we disobey and leave His protection, our sexual experiences start to affect our minds. One man who discovered this was a worker in a Christian ministry. He offered to drive me to the airport after a conference where I spoke. On the way there, he said:

> I need your help. I am married to one of the most wonderful women I have ever met. I love her and would do anything for her. But before I became a Christian, I was very active sexually. My sexual experiences became very bad. I would do anything to forget those sexual experiences I had before I met my wife.

When we have sex, the other women I have had in the past go through my mind. It is destroying my closeness with my wife. I am at the point where I do not want to have sex because I cannot stand remembering those things. The truth is, I have been married to this wonderful woman for eight years and I have never felt alone in the bedroom with her. Those other women always seem to be there with us.

Hebrews 13:4 teaches that the marriage bed is to be kept pure. "Pure" means to have no foreign material in it. Sex before or outside of marriage makes the marriage bed impure. We carry the memory of those other experiences into the marriage bed with us.

A young man came to me one time and said, " I used to be sexually involved and liked to look at sexual pictures. It has hurt our marriage. I still have to have the pictures. When I have sex with my wife, I cannot complete the sex act without a picture next to her head on the bed."

Some weeks later a woman told me that her feeling of self-worth had been destroyed. I asked her how. She said, "Every time my husband has sex with me, he has to have a sexual picture on the bed next to me. He cannot complete sex without it."

When a woman fears being compared with her husband's former lovers, she begins to wonder if she is good enough to compete. It creates insecurity, which comes from a feeling of being threatened.

Most young men think about sex and even picture it in their minds. That is also true of some young women. They fail to see the power of their thoughts on their sexual actions. They do not understand the power of their sexual actions on their thoughts. They do not understand that the way they live now has a direct effect on how they will live later.

God provides a way to freedom for those who have been sexually active and are troubled by it. Since He commands us to be changed in our minds, it must be possible for our minds to be made new.

It is hard to imagine that God can take away a bad memory, but He can. I remember being troubled by something out of my past. I knew God had forgiven me but I was not able to forget it. I prayed that God would take away that bad memory. Later I remembered making that prayer, but I could not remember what I had prayed about. The memory was gone.

So many of us need to bring our memories and past experiences under the rule of Jesus Christ. We need to allow Him to repair the damage. God always meets us right where we are and offers a fresh start. We need to begin today to build relationships that will leave good and godly memories.

God knows what is best for our minds. He has set up limits around sex to protect and provide for our minds.

Protection from Sex-controlled Relationships

When a male-female relationship is controlled by sex, the results can be terrible. A young woman wrote to tell me her sad story of sexual actions and lost love:

> My boyfriend was the only one I ever had sex with. I loved him and needed him. I wanted to keep him, but our social connection broke down. Soon we were fighting often. He thought it would help to have sex. I gave in because I wanted him to love me. We both got really selfish. We stayed together, but all the love was gone from the relationship.

The marriage relationship is meant to last a lifetime. To make that possible, people need to get to know each other in the time leading up to marriage. They need to spend time together and learn about each other. When the growing closeness between them leads to marriage, they can know what they are getting. After they are married, they are free to confirm the relationship as only a husband and wife can.

Sex before marriage stops the growth of those things that must be present for a marriage to work. Anyone can kiss, but not everyone can have a meaningful talk with another person. Often a relationship that starts sex too soon is never able to reach the deeper closeness of mind and spirit. If we stay within God's limits, we are protected.

Protection from Damaged Family Relationships

People who have sex before marriage are more likely to have sex outside of marriage. Sex can be a way to feel good immediately when problems come. It makes the problems go away for a short time. Later when sex with the husband or wife leaves problems unsolved, tenseness comes into the marriage. They begin to pull back from each other physically and emotionally. One or both may go looking for the "good feeling" they had enjoyed before with another person.

By saying that we must wait until marriage for sex, God protects us from these hurtful relationships. He wants sex in marriage to be a way of making our relationship stronger. His wisdom is greater than all our excuses.

One of God's provisions for sex within marriage is the blessing of children. A marriage is complete without children, but as the father of four children I know the great joy children bring to a marriage. Sex before marriage can damage relationships with the children that are later born in marriage.

When an unmarried woman becomes pregnant, both she and the man have a number of possibilities. First they can have a quick marriage because they feel responsible. These marriages do not have to fail, but they begin with guilt and pressure. This can cause two people to begin a family when they are not mature enough for that responsibility.

A second possibility is to give the baby to a man and woman who are married. This is often the most loving thing to do, especially if the mother and father are too young to raise their child.

A third possibility is for the mother to keep the child even if she does not marry. If the mother who does that is very young, there is a good chance that she will be poor all her life.

A fourth possibility is to kill the child before it is born. That may be the quickest way to escape the problem, but it hurts the mother physically, emotionally and spiritually. Future children can continue to remind the parents of the child that was killed. For the rest of her life the mother will remember that child. That also will be felt by her living children.

Young people who want to please their parents by not having sex are under the protection of God's blessing. When they obey God's commands, they can become the special person God created them to be.

Protection from the Traps of Living Together

More than half of all first marriages are by people who live together before they are married. In a growing number of these marriages, the mother already has children.

Some people say that living together before marriage gives a man and a woman a way to really get to know each other. Then if they decide to get married, they will have a good and long-lasting marriage.[1] But one study of more than 13,000 people in 1992 shows that is not true. The study found that when people live together outside of marriage there is more conflict and less talking together.[2] Let us look at several areas where men and women living together outside of marriage have problems.

People who live together outside of marriage often have a problem talking together. They are afraid to really discuss the things that concern them. They are afraid that the other person will leave them.

People who live together outside of marriage often do not decide important things together. For example, money and property seem to be either his or hers, not theirs. If they marry, they know they will have to decide together how they are going to use their money.

People who live together outside of marriage often separate because they become unhappy with their sex lives. They are under no real pressure to work out their sexual problems together. One study found that "married people have sex more often with higher levels of satisfaction than people in any other kind of sexual relationship."[3]

People who live together outside of marriage usually are interested only in their personal gain. For example, in their relationship they may want friendship, sexual satisfaction or money. Those things have nothing to do with giving to another person or making a relationship stronger.

People who live together outside of marriage are no more likely to find the "right" person to marry than those who do not live together before marriage. The secret to a lasting marriage is for each person to work at making himself a better person. In that way, one can become the right person for another person to find.

Provision for a Very Special Relationship in Marriage

You would never want the following to be true of you:

> I never understood how I would feel cheated until the night we were married and got to our hotel room. I was getting ready for the most loving evening of my life. Then I thought, "Well, I have already done this. What is there to be excited about?" That thought took all the life out of me.

> Sex used to be so much fun before we got married. Now, when it should have been the greatest expression of love between a husband and a wife, it had no meaning. This was a problem for us for almost a year. It was about to destroy our marriage when we finally went to some close friends. They gave us good advice and prayed with us. Finally we felt that the Lord had forgiven us. Then things were as they should be.

God does not want a young person's marriage night to be just another time for sex. He wants it to be the beginning of a very special relationship between two people who have followed His will for sex. The special nature of sex within marriage is clearly seen when we remember what marriage is. It is a lifelong chance to minister to another person.

Provision of Being Sexually Pure

Lisa told me: "I am not sexually pure. Now that I have found the man I want to spend the rest of my life with, I wish I were. He is sexually pure, so we have talked about it and he accepts that I am not. We have decided not to have sex until after we are married. We feel good about that."

Sexual purity can be lost only once. When it is lost, it is gone forever. Many people feel some sadness when they lose it before

124

the marriage night. Even some people who do not believe in the Bible place great value on being sexually pure. That lets us know how important it really is. No wonder God wants to bless every family with this lovely gift. Part of God's provision for us is this thought: sexual purity is not something we lose in marriage; it is something we are free to give.

Provision of Love and Trust

A young woman wrote:

> Last July God gave me the most wonderful man in the world to be my husband. He is someone I can share my deepest feelings with. He is someone I can talk to God with. He is someone I know will always love me and be faithful to me. I am happy I waited for him.
>
> On the first night of our marriage, I experienced sex for the first time. It was with my husband. I would not have wanted to share my first time with any other man. I had no riches to offer my husband, but he did not ask for riches. All he wanted was me. That is just what I had to give him – all of me, untouched, his alone. That meant a great deal, and we both knew it.

As this shows, God has provided a powerful way for humans to show love to their husbands or wives. When we wait until the marriage night to have sex, we establish a meeting of trust and love that has no equal. Those who try to create love and trust outside of marriage fail terribly.

God's command is to limit sex to marriage. That command protects young people from hurting each other. It provides a situation in which they can express their love through sex.

Chapter 14

The Spiritual Reasons to Wait

Since it is God who commands us to keep sex for marriage, there are serious problems in our walk with God if we do not wait.

Protection from Spiritual Loss

Young people must understand the spiritual losses that come from sin. They must receive God's protection for their spiritual lives and growth by obeying Him.

Protection from a Sin Against the Body

The Bible says that sex before marriage is a sin against a person's own body. The Bible tells us that no other sin hurts the body as sex sin does. "The man who does a sex sin sins against his own body" (1 Corinthians 6:18). In other words, sex before marriage is a sin against God's purpose of purity for the human body.

God created each person as a whole being. He is interested in each of us as whole beings. Most importantly, He wants us to grow close to Him spiritually. But He also wants us to use our minds. He wants us to be in emotional health and physical health. He is interested in our conscience, our desires and our talk. He is interested in our social relationships and in our plans for the future. He is just as interested in our physical well-being and how we treat our bodies. If God tells us sex is wrong because it hurts our bodies, He knows what He is talking about.

Just as true love shows love for the whole person, false love in the form of sex before marriage hurts the whole person. It hurts our emotions and our mind. It keeps us from making godly judgments. Nothing is safe from the damage it can do.

Protection from God's Judgment

We read in Hebrews 13:4: "Marriage should be respected by everyone. God will punish those who do sex sins and are not faithful in marriage." As one student wrote:

> If we choose not to obey God, we place ourselves under His judgment. When we do that we will receive the results of living outside the limits He has set for us. Because we live in a sinful world, most young people find it hard to wait to experience sex. From everything I have heard and read, sex sounds great. That is why I believe it is worth waiting for!

Please remember that God's punishment comes from His love for us. It is like parents who punish disobedient children because they love them. God created us with the freedom to choose, but He has not left us without guidance. He has given us a value system to help us choose. If we choose what is within God's value system, blessings will come. If we go outside of His limits, we must suffer the results.

God's laws show His protection and provision for us. Those laws are not designed to help one person more than another. God understands our weakness, but He does not listen to excuses. Sooner or later, those who disobey His laws will pay the price.

Protection from Broken Friendship

Sin builds a wall between us and God. Isaiah 59:2 says, "But your wrong doings have kept you away from your God. Your sins have hidden His face from you, so that He does not hear." Since the Bible is firm about keeping sex for marriage, a young person who chooses to have sex outside of marriage will be fighting against God. One young person put it this way:

Believe me, there are bad results from purposely disobeying God. I went through much unnecessary pain and sorrow when I separated myself from the Lord. I should have obeyed the Word of the Lord. I discovered that everything in Scripture is completely necessary to us.

Sexual sin will cause a person to lose his desire for spiritual things. Jesus said, "Everyone who sins hates the Light. He stays away from the Light because his sin would be found out" (John 3:20). Everything that has to do with God points out our sins and guilt. So we begin to stay away from such things as prayer, Bible study and Spirit-filled preaching. After awhile, even though we know that what we are doing is wrong, we do not care. Then it is no longer possible to repent and return to Him apart from the grace of God.

When a Christian becomes involved in sex sin, he begins to feel uneasy with God. He is less likely to attend church, pray and read the Bible. You can see that in what this student wrote:

> Julie and her boyfriend were both brought up in Christian homes. There they learned that they should wait for marriage to have sex. They had heard from the "old people" that they would get carried away if they let their emotions get the best of them. But they both felt they could control their emotions.
>
> After going together for eight months, they began to touch each other sexually. About two years later they finally went all the way. At one time they had both been very close to God. Their sin hurt their relationship with Him very much. The feelings of guilt have been there ever since they started going too far.

God wants to protect young people from this. When God calls us to holiness and a daily walk with Him, He is doing it for our good.

128

Protection from Being a Bad Influence on Other Christians

The Bible says, "Live so that your Christian brother will not have a reason to trip or fall into sin because of you" (Romans 14:13). When a Christian has sex before marriage, it can cause another Christian to trip in his walk with the Lord. That can happen in at least three ways. First, a Christian who becomes sexually involved with a newer Christian will keep the newer Christian from growing spiritually. Second, a Christian who leads another Christian to do something they both know is wrong will damage that person's conscience. Third, a Christian can cause another Christian to trip just by his example.

The purpose of a relationship between two Christians should be to build each other up in the Lord. To decide if a relationship is good or not, each must ask, "Am I growing in my walk with the Lord through this? Is the other person growing closer to the Lord?" If the answer to either of those questions is no, the relationship is not good.

God protects us from the bad influence of others when He commands His followers not to cause one another to trip.

Protection from Being a Bad Influence on Non-Christians

One student had these wise words of advice about a Christian's witness to the world:

> As Christians, we are witnesses to non-Christians. As we go through life we need to remember that our actions will always speak louder than our words. Sex before marriage is a very "loud" action. It would not be good for our witness as Christians.

Perhaps there is no more tragic result of the sexual sin of Christians than its effect on non-Christians. When King David fell into sex sin, Nathan told him, "By this act you have given those who hate the Lord a reason to speak against the Lord" (2 Samuel 12:14).

I have known many young people who got involved with unbelievers in the hope of bringing them to Christ. Instead they became sexually involved with them. On the one hand, they were trying to witness. On the other hand, they were going the way of the non-Christian's life.

God knows that young people live in a fallen world. He knows that the temptations of the world are great. But He calls Christian young people to be witnesses for Him. He provides the means that will keep them pure: the Scriptures, the Holy Spirit and the body of believers.

Provision for Spiritual Blessing for Sexual Purity

"God wants you to be holy. You must keep away from sex sins. God wants each of you to use his body in the right way by keeping it holy and by respecting it. You should not use it to please your own desires like the people who do not know God" (1 Thessalonians 4:3-5). God's Word is clear. He allows no sex outside the marriage relationship. When young people keep sexual purity, they become useful paths for God's love. Then they can effectively show God to others.

Sexual purity protects us from the terrible results of hurting the holiness of sex. It protects us from misusing our body, the house of the Holy Spirit. It protects us from hurting our witness for Christ, allowing us to show Him as He is. It protects us from the pain Solomon described in Proverbs 6:27-28, when warning his son not to desire an evil woman: "Can a man carry fire in his arms, and his clothes not be burned? Can a man walk on hot coals, and his feet not be burned?"

By remaining sexually pure, young people enjoy the provision and the promise of God's blessings. That is true in their future sex lives in marriage as well as in many other areas of life.

Provision of the Blessing of Not Giving Up

Waiting for something builds excitement. The longer you wait, the greater your satisfaction will be when it finally comes. Not giving up is one of the fruits of the Spirit. Galatians 5:22-23 says: "But the fruit that comes from having the Holy Spirit in our lives is: love, joy, peace, not giving up, being kind, being good, having faith, being gentle, and being the boss over our own desires (self-control). The Law is not against these things."

Here is what a young person wrote to me about waiting: "Waiting will help one to keep his or her body's desires under the rule of Christ. This will develop self-control, an important fruit of the Holy Spirit."

What we are when the Holy Spirit works in our lives shows God's provision for us. When we have self-control, we will have goodness and peace. When we wait without giving up, we will have love and joy. When the Spirit works in our lives, God blesses us with such fullness that we can hardly receive it all. At the same time, the workings of the Spirit are there to protect us. God keeps us out of trouble when we keep our minds on Him.

Provision of the Blessing of Trust

God knows that marriages need to be built on trust. If we think there might be a possibility of unfaithfulness, that trust is hurt. One young person wrote about the element of trust in a relationship:

> When God presented me to Mr. Right, we worked fourteen months to save sex for marriage. We have now been married for three years. I have never been sorry

about the no's or the reasons for the no's. I firmly believe that waiting until marriage to experience sex can only make the marriage better. Our doing that created a trust that cannot be equaled. We both loved the Lord and each other so much that we wanted our first time to be with the one we loved for life.

God's command that we keep sex for marriage shows His love for us. He wants to protect us from the damaging effects that the lack of trust brings to a marriage. At the same time He wants to provide us with the best sex life possible.

A man described what he felt was the thinking of most young men:

> Most of the time when I found myself in bed with a woman, I wished it had never gone that far. After I reached a point where I knew I would be spending the night with her, there was no more enjoyment in it. I just went through the motions. There were times when all I wanted was to hurry up and finish it. I finally stopped having sex when I understood that sex is no good unless there is true trust and love involved.

Gretchen Kurz, a student at San Jose State University, finished a report with these words:

> With all that is being said about sexual freedom, it is a little hard to admit that it is not what everyone says it is. For that reason, here we sit, closed-mouth and too uneasy to say we could not find that freedom. We cannot admit it to the world or, worse yet, to ourselves. Perhaps we could all begin to set the record right by saying that without love and trust sex is just not worth the effort.[1]

132

In answering a question, my wife, Dottie, finished this way: "The reason I completely trust Josh is because he has a record of trust." The record was built over time.

Provision of Jesus to Fill the Emptiness

Many young people get into sex because they feel empty. God did not design sex to meet a person's deepest longings. Only Jesus does that. Those young people who promise to obey God's Word and wait for sex open themselves to the blessing of Christ's presence filling their emptiness. Here is what one young woman wrote after making that discovery:

> Since becoming a Christian, I have found that the spiritual emptiness I thought could be filled by another person can be filled only by Jesus Christ. I can feel a deep, satisfying love without sex. But also I can see that sex is the greatest way of showing love for another person other than dying for him or her. It is so great that it is to be shared only by those who have promised to love each other for the rest of their lives. I am thankful to be able to wait and share that closeness only with my husband.

Once we form a relationship with Christ, only we can break that relationship. God never turns His back on anyone. He never does anything to harm those He loves. This is something that cannot be said for even the best human relationship.

God did not have to create man in order to love. God is love. He created man so that man could enjoy the blessings of God's love. He did not create us in order to receive from us. He created us in order to give to us. He proved His love by sending Christ to save us. That was the greatest price that could be paid for another. It means that there is no limit to the value God places on each of us.

The Blessings of God-planned Sex

The world gives young people a false idea about the joys of sex. The real joys of sex come from doing it God's way. God created us. He made us to be sexual beings. He knows all about sex. He knows when we should have sex and when we should not have sex. As the Bible says, "There is a special time for everything. There is a time for everything that happens under heaven" (Ecclesiastes 3:1).

God's time for sex is marriage. When young people wait for God's time, they can expect and enjoy God's blessings.

Chapter 15
Why "Safe Sex" Is Not Safe

Amy Stephens writes:

> A doctor friend of mine called last week. He told me
> that that day he had to tell four women they had STDs
> that could not be cured. His next comment shocked me:
> "I spend hours in surgery treating STDs that cannot be
> cured. How can I tell my 17-year-old that sex is safe?"[1]

The safe-sex message of our culture gives a false sense of
security to young people. They think: *I want to have sex, but I
do not want to get pregnant or catch a disease. So I will do what
my health class teacher says to do. I will have safe sex by using
a condom.*

The only problem is that safe sex is not safe. At best, safe sex is
only safer sex. Yet condoms are often advised in schools. They
are even given to the students in some schools. Doctors warn
those who come to them, "If you are going to have sex before
marriage, protect yourself with a condom." Others say, "Not
having sex with a person who has STDs is the best way to keep
from getting an STD. But the Public Health Service also has
advised condom use."

When young people are told to use condoms, many of them think
that our culture approves of sex before marriage. The difference
between safe sex and safer sex can mean big trouble for some
young people.

Young people should wait for sex until marriage because safe sex
will not keep all of them safe from pregnancy or disease. God
wants to protect young people from a sense of false security. He
wants to provide real safety for them with His design of no sex
outside of marriage.

The Dangers of Condom Failure

The idea of safe sex is not new. It goes back to the time when birth-control medicine was first offered to the public. With that medicine people felt free to enjoy sex without the fear of getting pregnant. Medical experts did not know then that the freedom the medicine would provide would also bring so many STDs. Many sexually active people today do not understand that the birth-control medicine can do nothing to protect them from STDs.

Many experts agree that condoms are a dangerous way to have sex. Why? Because they can fail. They leak. They break. Some STDs are so small they can pass through the condoms.

Studies show that the failure rate for condoms is about 30 percent.[2] Think of this in human terms. For every ten students who have sex using a condom, three of them will experience condom failure. The condom will break, leak or fall off during the experience. These students are open to pregnancy and disease.

Many people believe that using both condoms and medicine will prevent or cure STDs. The great increase in STDs shows that is not true. Modern science finds that condoms provide no protection at all for several serious diseases. They provide very little protection for some other diseases. There are some STDs for which there is no cure. The only way to prevent a disease that cannot be cured is to stay away from it. The only effective way to do that is to have no sex until marriage and then marry someone who has done the same.

Dr. John Diggs of the Family Research Council says:

> Condoms are the most important part of the idea of safe sex. The truth is that the three most common STDs are passed from one person to another at about the same rate as if no condoms were used.

136

It is true that condoms do stop HIV and gonorrhea part of the time if condoms are used every time a person has sex. There are two problems with that. First, most people do not use a condom every time. Second, even if people do use condoms every time, some of them will still get HIV or gonorrhea. In the case of gonorrhea, this is not very serious. But HIV kills. Although death can take years, it will surely come. In the meantime, the person with HIV can give it to others.

Three other STDs hurt millions of Americans each year. Two of these have no cure. The sad thing is that this is all the result of people thinking it is all right to have sex with anyone and everyone. These problems could be completely prevented if sex were limited to marriage.

One wonders why groups that are responsible for protecting our health have chosen not to tell young people how condoms fail. The answer, I believe, is that they fear asking people to change their actions. Condoms are the "easy" answer. They cost little and can be carried easily. But they do not work. People need to see that what God says about sex is really true. Sex should be saved for marriage.[3]

The following was taken from a piece on the Internet called "Do Condoms and Seat Belts Lead People to Take More Chances?"

Seat belts and condoms are two safety tools that are said to reduce danger and save lives. Three British men who have studied this ask an interesting question: "Is it possible that some people using these safety tools take more chances? Do they drive faster or have sex with more people because of an increased feeling of safety?"[4]

That is a good point. The safe-sex idea has become more popular among young people when schools and health groups hand out free condoms. In effect, health officials and teachers are saying to young people, "We know you are going to have sex. Protect yourself. Take these condoms with our good wishes."

Studies have shown that handing out condoms has failed. With condoms so easy to get, some students who have sex have it more often. Students who have not had sex are tempted to experiment. It gives young people a false sense of security. Consider the following report of what happened when condoms were handed out in high schools in San Francisco, St. Paul and Dallas:

> San Francisco: Students were shown pictures of the correct way to use a condom. Still the Balboa High School condom program turned out to be a huge failure. Pregnancy increased by one-fourth. This would also mean a similar increase in the number of students who might have an STD.

> St. Paul and Dallas: In two school-based programs that handed out condoms . . . the results were even worse than those in San Francisco. A St. Paul program that was expected to reduce pregnancies among students really caused them to increase by one-third. A Dallas school that handed out condoms ended up with a pregnancy rate 47 percent higher than another school very much like it that did not hand out condoms. It is foolish to believe that handing out condoms to young people might work better if experts tell them how to use them. Strong condom teaching has proven to be a complete failure.[5]

Is Virginity the Same as Abstinence?

One of the reasons it is so important to teach the meaning of true abstinence is that virgins can get STDs. That is because people can remain virgins if they do not complete the sex act between a male and a female. Two boys being sexually active together are still virgins. The same is true of two girls.

"Virgin" is when a boy has not entered into a girl or a girl has not been entered into by a boy. "Abstinence" is when a boy or girl is not sexually active. That is, there is no sexual activity between any two people before marriage.

Studies show the importance of complete abstinence until marriage. It is the only way to protect against STDs. In addition, the abstinence message is needed because it works and because it is God's plan for all people. Without God's rules about sex, young people can suffer all the hurtful effects of sex before marriage. Telling the whole story would mean teaching young people about the emotional effects of sex before marriage. There is no condom for the heart.[6]

The only safe and healthy sexual way for young people is sexual abstinence. Recent increases in the numbers of young people who are abstinent show that sexual abstinence is not just healthy, it is possible. Abstinence is more than a religious issue. It is an issue of personal and public health.[7]

Provision of Virginity

In the past younger Americans have not accepted their parents' idea that sex before marriage is wrong. That difference is becoming less as the abstinence message becomes more widely accepted. In Atlanta, Georgia, a group called Families First has placed signs along roads saying, "Virgin: Teach your child it is not a bad word." Similar messages are being put on television.[8]

Many people believe that messages like these are beginning to help across the nation. A 1995 study of more than 500 high school students shows that 62 percent of sexually experienced girls said they "should have waited."[9] Many boys agreed. A 1996 report found that even among those young people who had had sex 25 percent were now abstinent.

Abstinence until marriage, followed by one husband or wife in marriage, is God's perfect plan for safe sex. It is His loving provision for us and our children. It may not be popular in many places, but it works. That is shown by the following story told to me by a friend:

> A local school committee on rules invited parents of their high school students in to discuss the school's sex-education program. After much of the material had been presented, one of the parents said, "There is not enough importance put on abstinence." The speaker joked about that and everyone laughed.
>
> A few minutes later, the group took a break for rolls and coffee. These parents felt they would not be welcome to mix with the rest of the parents, so they stayed in their places.
>
> Following the break, the leader said, "Please look on the back of the paper you are wearing that tells your name. One of them has a flower." The person with the flower raised his hand.
>
> Then the leader said, "Will those who shook hands with this man please stand?" Nearly everyone stood. Then the leader said, "Everyone who shook hands with any of those who are standing please stand." Only the parents who advised teaching abstinence did not stand.
>
> Then the leader said, "Let us say that the person with the flower has an STD. Now, all of you have the same STD. That is how quickly it can spread."
>
> The parents who had advised abstinence said, "We did not shake hands with any of the rest of you. In your story we do not have the STD. We advise abstinence. We accept your story and rest our case."[10]

In this part of the book we have considered a number of reasons why young people should say no to sex before marriage. In the rest of the book we will explore several ways to help young people make the promise to wait for sex until marriage and to help them keep that promise.

Chapter 16
Develop a Caring Relationship With Your Children

In this chapter we will consider ways to help young people stand against a culture that is pushing them into having sex before marriage. This student says it well: "I think it is time young people get the love they need at home instead of in the back seat of an old car."

The first important step to save your children from having sex before marriage is to have a strong love in the home. That love must be between Father and Mother and between parent and child. God established the family as a way of showing what He is like. When families fight or separate, the children have a hard time understanding God's love. God wants the family to point a child to perfect love, to God Himself.

A Christian's relationship with God is based on trust. In the same way a child needs to be able to have perfect trust in his parents. A Christian is secure in his relationship with God. A child should have that same security in his relationship with his parents. Just as in our relationship with God, children learn to love their parents because the parents first love them.

One large study found that "males born to mothers younger than 18 grow up to be almost three times more likely to be criminals than the sons of women who wait until age 20 to have their first child."[1]

Michael Dye said, "Young mothers are more likely to be unmarried and weak. They are not able to give and receive love." He goes on to say, "We learn caring from our mothers, but young mothers have not learned to love themselves." Dye also said that fathers give children "a sense of who they are. They give them purpose and goals."[2] Dye should know what he is talking about. He is a director of Bethel House and Santa Barbara Rescue Mission.

As parents, we need to spend more time with our children, whatever the cost. We need to know that

- if our children cannot talk to us, they will talk to other children.
- if we do not spend time with them, they will spend more time with other children.
- if they do not find closeness at home, they will seek it among other children.
- if they do not get loving touches from their fathers, they will get them from other children.
- if their parents will not listen to them, other children will.
- young people like relationships. That is why they like other young people so much.

A Good Parent-Child Relationship Leads to Less Sexual Involvement

Danny was an intelligent Christian young man who had come to me for advice. "Sometimes I feel so alone. I feel like no one cares about me. My mother and father live in their own world and I live in mine." He looked past me as he spoke more slowly. "It did not always seem that way. I know it sounds foolish, but I want them to leave me alone, and yet I want to be part of their lives. Most of the time, they do leave me alone and it gets very lonely."[3]

The biggest reason for young people's sexual crisis is their feeling of being separated from their parents. As parents provide the emotional, spiritual and mental strength for their child in a loving relationship, closeness will increase. Then the temptation to seek closeness through sexual involvement will become less.

There are five things I would like to share with you that may help you develop a closer parent-child relationship.

Let Them Know They Are Accepted

Our children need to know that whatever happens we will always love and accept them. This will give them the sense of security they need very much in today's world. Sometimes parents accept a child based on how the child acts. As long as the child does what the parents say, they will accept him. But if the child fails, the parents' love and accepting is taken away, for a time at least.

One way to show children they are always accepted is to praise them for what they try to do even if they are not able to do it.

Give Them Much Praise

Giving praise for who your child is gives him a sense of importance. Children need to know that their parents are thankful for who they are. As our children were growing, our aim was to try to catch them doing something good. When we found something, we were quick to praise them.

Be honest with your praise. Most children know when praise is not real. If you look closely, you should be able to find many good things to give true praise for.

Be There for Your Children

When you are there for your children, it gives them a sense of importance and worth. Simply put, if you spend time with your children, they will feel important because they see themselves as an important part of your life. This will also bring you good in the future. As my wise wife says, "If we spend time with our children now, they will spend time with us later. If we show an interest in them now, they will show an interest in us later."

144

Here are a few ideas for making and spending time with your young people. Allow them to stay up an hour later than usual sometimes and spend that time with them. Talk, play games, or do whatever might interest them.

Ask your young person to go with you when you need to go some place. That is a good time to talk. Take your young person out to eat, or go shopping together. Go some place where you can sit and watch people go by. Watch for unusual people. They will help you see what your child thinks is humorous, happy or sad.

Children need to know that they are more important to us than anything we might be doing when they need us.

Show Your Love

Children cannot get too much love, even in their high school years. They need to hear "I love you" over and over. They also need much touching, such as kisses and rubs. It is never too late to start. Another part of love is just having fun with your children. When they see that you are having fun and are glad to be with them, it makes them feel sure of your love. It frightens me when I think how little love children of 15 are getting at a time when they really need more love.

Establish Responsibility With Your Children

Establishing responsibility in your relationship with your children will give them a sense of responsibility. I am not talking here only about letting your children be responsible to you. That is only half of the story. It is also good to make yourself responsible to them. I have asked my children to help me be the best parent I can be by pointing out areas where I can improve.

One time I asked my children to write down five ways they wanted others to treat them. The number one thing they wrote was "kindness." I read Matthew 7:12 (the Golden Rule) to them.

Then I said that if they wanted others to treat them with kindness, they should start by being kind to others.

I also have tried to help my children understand that how we treat others relates to our relationship with God. One day when I went to the store with Sean, I did not do a very good job of parking the car. I took up parts of two parking spaces instead of one. I backed the car out and parked the right way. I said to Sean, "Do you know why I did that? If I took up both parking spaces, another person who wanted to go to this store would have to park a long way away. That would not be very loving of me, would it?" Things like that really stay in my children's minds. They help them see that I am responsible to God for how I treat other people as well as how I treat them.

When these five elements are built into your relationship with your young people, it will make the relationship a strong and healthy one.

Building Your Child's Self-Worth Leads to Less Sexual Involvement

One of the main reasons young people get involved in sex before marriage is that they have a poor self-worth. One young man tells how he used sex before marriage to increase his self-worth: "When a girl looked at me, that proved to me my worth as a male. As I got more involved with girls, I found it more difficult to stop and my life became filled with guilt."

Young women with low self-worth tell similar stories. They become sexually involved to "prove" their worth. Other young people become sexually involved as a way to make their poor opinion of themselves even poorer. They are acting out what they believe to be true about themselves.

In Romans 12:3 Paul said, "I ask each one of you not to think more of himself than he should think. Instead, think in the right way toward yourself by the faith God has given you." True lowliness of mind is knowing who we are as God sees us. It is accepting ourselves as we are and giving God the glory.

There are four things we should remember about how we think about ourselves. First, the Bible tells us that God made man and woman as the high point of creation. Second, the biblical picture of how much God values you is shown by His giving His Son to save you from the punishment of your sins.

Third, each of us is different. God created you to be you, and no one can be you better than you can. Finally, the biblical way of how we should see ourselves is that we are loved and accepted by God. God tells us, "I have loved you with a love that lasts forever" (Jeremiah 31:3). He accepts us just the way we are. The minute we put our trust in Jesus Christ as Savior and Lord we are accepted into God's family. We belong.

Building a healthy self-worth in your young people involves three main elements. The first element is a sense of belonging or a feeling of being loved just as I am. It is knowing that someone really cares for me.

The second element is a feeling of worth. Feeling worthy means feeling whole and good about yourself on the inside. It is a sense that you have earned the love and acceptance of others. One of the most important things you can do to help your children feel worthy is to be careful how you correct them. Correcting a child for bad actions will lead to a healthy self-worth. Correcting a child for being a "bad child" leads to a poor self-worth. We all have to correct our children. But when we do, we should be careful to correct the action, not the person. Even when you are correcting your children, show your love for them.

The third element in building a healthy self-worth is having a feeling of being able to do something well. As children grow, they need to understand that they can meet new tasks and hard things the right way. Here are three ways you can help your young person develop a sense of being able:

First, help your child find at least one thing that he can do especially well. If a child can feel especially good about one area, it will largely make up for not being able to do other things well. After finding that area, help him to improve in it. Praise him for it.

Second, help your child develop a sense of being able by helping him try great things and go for big dreams. That is especially true in things that serve others. I really believe that those who most enjoy life and have the best self-worth are those who have a dream of what they want to be and have given their lives to reaching that dream. It is much easier for children to go for worthy goals if their parents are cheering for them. Helping your child find areas where he can do well also will give him a sense of control of his life.

Third, each person is a special and different creation of God. He is the object of God's personal care and wonderful love. If you can help your child understand that, then you will have done much to make your child ready to choose a pure life.

Talking With Your Child Leads to Less Sexual Involvement

Being able to talk with your child is an important part of building a loving relationship. If you cannot talk to your young person, you will have difficulty developing a close relationship. You will not be able to build his self-worth. That is even more true if he cannot talk with you.

Many young people today are crying out for a real talk with a parent. They want a talk that involves not only the exchange of thoughts but also of feelings. If young people feel they are being laughed at when they speak, they will not want to share their real feelings or opinions. If every talk ends in an argument, they will stop talking.

148

Jesus said, "Let the little children come to Me. Do not stop them. The holy nation of heaven is made up of ones like these" (Matthew 19:14). It takes effort, but parents need to listen for the feelings behind the words. This is possible if we give our young people time for their real feelings to come out. Part of talking together is listening with our eyes as well as with our ears. If you watch for quiet signs, you will catch a great deal more of the talk.

Talking together is important to show love to our young people. It is also necessary to help them deal with their own sexuality.

How can you help your young people talk? How can you talk better with your young people? The following rules have helped me over the years as I have worked at becoming a better talker with my wife.

1. Work at it. We need to make an effort to talk better with our children. Some parents plan for a meal out together (maybe just a father and his daughter) now and then. Some go on a hunting trip together or a long ride in the car. Other ideas include:

- running, cooking, attending an evening meeting of some kind
- planning things to discuss at dinner or during rides together
- inviting your young person into your bedroom to talk or asking if you can come into his
- asking his opinions and giving real thought to those opinions

2. Try to understand. One of the ways to develop closeness is to let the other person know that you are trying to understand and that you truly care. This will cause both of you to be more open in the relationship. If a child feels that a parent does not want to listen or understand, it affects the child's self-worth. Parents need to see how their children are thinking. Young people may not take things the same way as older people do, so we need to talk to them in ways they will understand.

3. Do something to show that you are listening. It is easy to allow our minds to think about other things when another person is talking. Your young person will be more ready to talk with you if he can see that you are really listening to him. Here are some ways you can show your interest:

- Use your body. Turn toward your child. Move your head to show understanding. Keep looking into his eyes. Nothing shows interest more than the eyes do.
- Ask questions. When you ask a question, you are saying, "I am interested and want to understand."
- React to what he has said by saying something like, "That must have been hard for you."
- Show honest feelings when you repeat something that has been said. That makes things clear and leads to more talking.
- Remain silent when your child is telling a story. You may cut off something important.
- Try not to think of your answer while your child is talking. It makes you want to speak.

4. Help your child feel good about himself. The very act of listening gives a sense of value, worth and love. It makes your child feel important. Tell your child every day: "I love you." "You are special to me." "You make me so proud."

5. Look at the good side of things instead of the bad side. Look for the good things about your child and talk about those.

6. Keep their secrets. When your young people know that you are able to keep things to yourself, they feel a greater willingness to tell you things. If you disappoint your child, apologize – but remember next time.

7. Wait for the right time. Proverbs 15:23 says, "To give a good answer is a joy to a man, and how pleasing is a word given at the right time." In any relationship, talking together will be helped if it comes at the right time. Love must be your guide as to when and where you share bad news or discuss a difficult thing with your children. One parent told the following:

> One morning my son got off to a bad start. He took up his things and started for the door. I saw that he had not made his bed, fed his cat or put away his clothes. I spoke roughly to him as he went out the door. He gave me a bad look and ran for the bus. I felt so bad. What a way to send a child off to school. He was late. He might miss the bus and be late for school. Was that the right time to speak about those things?

There are three especially important times when you should choose your words carefully: when your child is going out the door, when your child first comes home from school, and when your child is ready to go to bed.

8. Share your feelings. In talking with your child, learn to say how you feel as well as what you think. If he knows you are willing to be hurt too, he may be more willing to be open about what he is feeling. Sometimes parents hide their feelings so that they will not get into an argument. But that usually creates pressures that will cause feelings to come out in other ways. Some parents use their feelings in a way that makes their children feel guilty. That usually makes the children talk less.

9. Be open. Do not expect your child to know what you are feeling. Speak up. Every relationship would be better and more close if we would just start telling how we feel.

10. Learn to compromise. A healthy relationship with your growing young people is a give-and-take situation. That does not mean that a parent has to be weak about rules and what is expected. As young people grow and show themselves to be responsible, they should be given more freedom and responsibility. It is sometimes hard to keep up with how they are growing, but it is important to change the rules as the young people change. That will keep them from rebelling against rules that are designed for younger children.

11. Be honest. Paul saw the issue clearly when he told us "to hold to the truth with love in our hearts" (Ephesians 4:15). This means to consider the other person's feelings. Keep your talking simple and direct. Part of being honest is your willingness to ask your children to forgive you when you are wrong. If we can admit when we are wrong, the damage can be taken care of. Trust can be established again.

Begin Today

Learning to talk with your children does not happen overnight, but you can start today. Every effort goes a long way toward telling your children that they are important. Good talking will help establish the base for a lifelong family relationship. It also will help your children deal with sexual pressure.

Chapter 17
Urge a Close Relationship With Christ

The human need for close, satisfying relationships is a real one. Doctors who treat the mind tell us that the greatest human need is to love and be loved. We long to share ourselves completely with another person. We want love and closeness, but we do not know how to find them. This is true for both young people and older people.

Sexual closeness alone can never fill a young person's deep need for closeness. However, there is a way to have lasting love and a closeness that does meet our deepest needs. The way to that closeness is in a personal relationship with Jesus Christ. He is the only one who always loves us with a perfect love.

You can help your children say no to sex before marriage by helping them toward a personal relationship with Jesus. As their closeness with Him grows, your young people will be less likely to seek sexual closeness.

Establishing a Relationship With Christ

Here are four points that can change your life:

First, God loves you perfectly and wants to give you the best in all areas of your life. That includes your sex life.

Second, we all have the problem of self. That leads us to push the limits of God's commands. The Bible calls that sin and says that there are punishments for sin. One of the punishments for sin is not to experience all the good things God wants to give us. Another punishment is separation from God. The Bible says we cannot take care of that separation by ourselves.

Third, God has solved the problem of separation by sending Jesus to die for us. By doing that He paid the price for our sins.

153

Then Jesus was raised from the dead to give us new life. He opened the way to God so that we can experience God's perfect love for us.

Fourth, we each have to choose to accept or reject what God has already provided for us. If we reject it, we can continue searching for true closeness, but we will not find it. If we accept God's way, God will fill our need for love and closeness as we experience His perfect love and plan for our lives.

If you would like to enter into this close relationship with God through His Son, pray the following prayer:

> Dear Jesus, I need You. I know I am a sinner and cannot help myself. Thank You for dying on the cross to pay the price for my sins. I want to have a close relationship with You. Please forgive my sins, come into my life as my Savior and fill my heart with Your love. Thank You for forgiving my sins and giving me eternal life. Help me to live for You from now on, and make me the kind of person You want me to be.

After you begin a relationship with Jesus, you need to develop that relationship. In order to be able to say no to sex, you need to develop and keep up a close walk with God. Here is what one young person says about this very necessary relationship:

> It is important to stay in a close relationship with Jesus. If we start pulling away from Jesus, we are too weak to fight against our sexual feelings. If your relationship with God is not right, then no other relationship can be right either. If both you and your boyfriend are right with God, it is so much easier to get help from Him when you need it.

Developing a close walk with Christ will do at least three important things for you:

154

First, it will fill your need for closeness. Your relationship with God is like a growing love. You will not feel so lonely, so you will no longer need to fill that emptiness in your life in a sexual way.

Second, as you develop a closer relationship with God, there will be a growing desire to please Him. Out of love for God, you will want to do what He commands. That includes no sex before marriage.

Third, you will have the power of God to help you fight against temptation. First Corinthians 10:13 promises us, "You have never been tempted to sin in any different way than other people. God is faithful. He will not allow you to be tempted more than you can take. But when you are tempted, He will make a way for you to keep from falling into sin."

Dealing with Temptation

It takes lowliness of mind to admit that we have a problem with something. When we think we can deal with sexual temptation on our own, though, we are just setting ourselves up for failure. A young person says:

> Young people often find themselves in situations where they cannot say no. So many times we say, "Oh, I can deal with it if I am ever in that situation." We do not stop before going into something. Instead we try to stop in the middle. It is like reading a good book. Once you have started, it is hard to put it down. Sex is the same way. Once you have begun, it is hard to stop.

The first step to keep from sinning is to admit to yourself and to God that you are weak. When you admit your weakness, you feel the need to stay away from situations where you will be tempted. You depend upon God's strength through the Holy Spirit instead of on your own strength.

The best way to keep your mind free of tempting thoughts is to keep your mind on God's Word. Psalm 119:9 says, "How can a young man keep his way pure? By living by Your Word."
It is very important to your sexual purity to keep reading the Bible. Learn parts of it by memory. Talk about the Bible with other people. Spend some time with God's Word every day. It will protect you.

Whatever you think about will direct your actions. Every temptation begins with something we see or hear, and that produces a thought. As the mind continues to think about it, a decision to act on that thought is formed. Our culture talks about sex so much that you will not be able to close your eyes and ears completely to the issue. If you listen to our culture, your mind will be filled with thoughts of sex. Then it is only a short step to getting involved in sex. There is only one way to keep that from happening. That is to control your mind.

When temptation comes, you must deal with it immediately. Do not let it settle down in your mind and stay there. One way to control the mind is to choose what goes into it. For example, it is much easier to stop sexual temptation when you are reading the Bible than when you are looking at sexual pictures. One student wrote about this:

> I am not the kind of person that keeps good control of my thoughts and actions. But I read the Bible every night even if I am very tired or it is late. I also make sure that I pray before getting into bed. After making that promise to myself nearly a year ago, I am amazed at how God's wonderful grace has protected me. "Think as Christ Jesus thought" (Philippians 2:5).

It is difficult to have a sinful desire or impure thought when your mind is fixed on Jesus. One reason is that Jesus Himself had no sinful desires or impure thoughts. If you want to say no to sexual temptation, fix your thoughts on Jesus. Colossians 3:2 says: "Keep your minds thinking about things in heaven. Do not think about things on the earth."

Pleasing Christ

Scripture tells us that we cannot serve two masters (Matthew 6:24). That is especially true in the area of sex. We cannot follow both the desires of our bodies and the Holy Spirit, who calls us to be sexually pure. Our sexual desires tell us to please ourselves. God's Spirit calls us to please Him. In this battle between our body and His Spirit, we must choose to please the Lord instead of ourselves. A student wrote:

> WAIT! If you love that person you are dating, wait! If you expect to love the person you will marry some day, wait! If you love God, wait! If you love, you will wait because "love does not give up, . . . love never thinks of itself" (1 Corinthians 13:4-5). Why wait until marriage to have sex? For love. That is why.

As you think on God's Word and try to please Him, you will become more like Him. Your life will show the fruit of His Holy Spirit: "love, joy, peace, not giving up, being kind, being good, having faith, being gentle, and being the boss over your own desires" (Galatians 5:22-23).

Christ Accepts You Just As You Are

A personal relationship with Christ fills your deep need for closeness. It also meets your need for complete acceptance. True acceptance comes only from God. He created you, not because He needed you, but because He wanted you.

We truly need God. In Him we live and have fullness of life, both now and forever. It is we who are helped by a relationship with God, not Him. When we know that, we see how valuable we are in God's eyes. Everything He does, He does for us. God calls you to walk with Him for your own good.

God considers each of us so important that He sent His Son to pay the price for our sins. He also opened the door to our relationship with Him. All we have to do is answer His offer of love. With a love so accepting and complete, how can we refuse?

You are loved for who you are, not for what you do. That is why true acceptance can come only from God. All people need the healthy sense of worth God means for them to have. It is found in Romans 12:3 where Paul says, "I ask each one of you not to think more of himself than he should think. Instead, think in the right way toward yourself by the faith God has given you." We need to keep in mind that all we have and all we are able to do are gifts from God. Every good thing comes from God (James 1:17).

Living in the Power of the Holy Spirit

Another very necessary element to saying no to sexual temptation is the ministry of the Holy Spirit in our lives. The following publication, written by my friend Chuck Klein, clearly explains the ministry of God's Spirit.

> One of the most important things in learning to say no to sex before marriage is learning to say yes to the Holy Spirit's leading in our lives. Only one person has ever lived a perfect life. That is Jesus Christ. Now, by His Spirit, He wants to live that life through us.

> God's design for sex is to protect and please us. But let us be honest. His plan is beyond our power. God never asks something of us without giving us the possibility of doing it. How does God do this? A Christian is someone who has the Holy Spirit in him. First Corinthians 3:16

asks us, "Do you not know that you are a house of God and that the Holy Spirit lives in you?" If you have received Christ, God's Spirit (the Holy Spirit) lives in you right now.

The Holy Spirit makes us new people in Christ. He gives us the tools to deal with serious pressures and problems, like the big issue of sex! God wants us to use our free will by obeying His Spirit. He wants us to let Him give us His power to attack our sexual problems. Where the Holy Spirit is producing His goodness in us, we have freedom to experience God's kind of relationships. There is power to say no and to wait.[1]

How can we give the Holy Spirit control of our lives? There are four steps.

First, confess your sins. The Bible says, "If we tell Him our sins, He is faithful and we can depend on Him to forgive us our sins. He will make our lives clean from all sin" (1 John 1:9). If you want to make things right with God, take time right now to list the things you know you should confess. Agree with God about those things through prayer. Then thank God for His forgiveness.

Second, know God's will. God wants us to be filled by His Spirit. Ephesians 5:18 says, "Be filled with the Holy Spirit." If God's will is for us to be Spirit-filled, what should we do next? First John 5:14-15 tells us, "We are sure if we ask anything that He wants us to have, He will hear us. If we are sure He hears us when we ask, we can be sure He will give us what we ask for." When we ask God for something that He means for us to have, He is going to give it to us.

Third, ask for His filling. God wants you to come to Him in lowliness of mind and ask Him to fill you with His Spirit. You may or may not feel any different after God's Spirit takes control.

Remember, God works in our lives because we put our faith in the facts of His Word. When it comes to our sexual lives, we must have the loving influence of God's Spirit.

Fourth, follow His leading. You have to decide to give the Holy Spirit control of your life. Then as the days pass, God's Spirit will take more and more control. But be careful. You must always cooperate with God's Spirit. If you fall, let God pick you up. We have to choose to turn from the things like bad pictures that damage our sexual lives and our relationship with Christ. If we are willing to turn, God's Spirit makes it possible for us to turn. Where the Spirit is in control, we find power and freedom.

Relationships are needed to help your young people say no to sex before marriage. They will be helped greatly by a loving, helping relationship with parents. But a close relationship with Christ and His Spirit are even more important.

Chapter 18
Teach Sexual Values at Home

Parents have the greatest responsibility for keeping young people from becoming sexually involved. It must be parents who love them. It must be parents whose lives and marriage they approve and want to be like.

If my children come to me with a sexual issue and I feel they are thinking about doing something they should not, I ask them three questions: (1) Do you know I love you? (2) Do you know I love your mother? (3) When you get married and have love and sex and children, do you want your family to be like our family? This last question is very important.

If they answer yes to all three of those questions, I have the perfect base to influence their thoughts and actions. The more help we give our children by the example we show them, the more they will be able to choose right.

How to Be a Good Example

Children need to see working examples of what a marriage should be. If they do not have that example in the home, later they will leave a relationship as soon as they meet with conflict.

The relationship children have with their parents is the first thing that will keep them from giving in to the pressures to have sex before marriage. Another very important thing is the relationship they see between their father and mother. It takes secure children to say no to pressure. A great deal of that security comes from knowing that the relationship between their parents is secure. One of the greatest things I can do for my children is to love their mother.

It is interesting that the Scripture we like to repeat to our children is," Children, as Christians, obey your parents. This is the right thing to do" (Ephesians 6:1). That comes immediately after Ephesians 5:33. There Paul tells each husband to "love his wife as he loves himself. Every wife must respect her husband." Security in the home comes when a husband and wife love each other and show it. When the father and mother honor each other, the children learn to obey.

The Need to Be an Example of Love

Most young people who get involved in sex before marriage are not really looking just for sex. They want closeness. They want to talk together, to understand and be understood. They want to love and be loved. Young people used to receive the love and security they needed from their parents and their brothers and sisters. Today, however, families are falling apart.

My wife, Dottie, has discovered an important difference in Ephesians 5:33. While the first need of a woman is love, the first need of a man is respect. Love meets a woman's deepest need. Men seem to want to be respected as the provider and protector of the home. So when I talk about showing love, I am talking mainly to husbands. When I talk about showing respect, I am talking mainly to wives.

How can we be examples of love and respect? Mainly, love and respect need to be spoken. Children need to hear their father say to their mother, "I love you." They need to hear their mother say to their father, "I believe in you."

Our daughter Kelly used to speak without respect to her mother. One time when I was home, I heard her speaking that way. I sat Kelly down in a chair. Then I got down on one knee and looked her in the eye. "Young lady," I said," you might talk to your mother that way, but I will never let you talk to my wife that way! I love that woman."

That one firm message made Kelly stop talking that way. A few months later she started to talk that way to Dottie again. But she caught herself and said to me, "Oh, I cannot do that to your wife, can I?"

Another way I show my love for Dottie in front of our children is by leaving little love notes for her to find. Dottie really enjoys these reminders of my love. The children enjoy watching her find them. Another idea is to involve your children in helping plan special times for your wife or husband.

Here is a list of ways wives say their husbands show love.

- He starts family prayer time.
- He tells the family that "my wife is a special person."
- He is quick to forgive. He shows unconditional love and acceptance.
- He makes sure that I have time for myself and for the Lord.
- He remembers special days.
- He looks at me when I talk to him and remembers what I say.
- He shares his feelings with me and shows his trust.
- He loves our children and sees the little things they do.
- He praises me on special things and takes note when I work hard at something.
- He helps me with little things like cleaning off the table after a meal.
- He nurses me when I am sick.
- He loves my family and takes an interest in them.
- He seems to know when I am sad and treats me with special kindness.

Here is a list of ways husbands say their wives show respect.

- She tells me she trusts me.
- She honors me in public and praises me in front of our children.
- She makes time for me and offers her time to do the things I want to do.
- She seeks my advice.
- She does not criticize me in public.
- She listens carefully.
- She says that she loves and respects me.
- She backs me by telling others that they might seek me out for advice or help.
- She gives me freedom and respects my private time.
- She holds a high opinion of who I am, what I do, and what I say.
- She prepares the meals I like best.
- She allows me to dream and set goals and helps me reach those goals.

The Difficulties of Being an Unmarried Parent

If you are an unmarried parent, you have an especially hard job. You do not have a helper with whom you can be an example of a strong, loving relationship. You do not even have the hope of making a bad marriage good. What can you do?

There is no easy answer. There are only three things I can tell you. First, even more than the married parent, you need to give your child much love and time. Plan interesting things to do and discuss with them.

Second, if your husband is still alive but you are no longer married, talk to your children about what marriage can be. Do not be afraid to admit the mistakes you have made.

Third, show by both your actions and your words that marriage is the only correct place for a sexual relationship. You yourself have to hold back from the pressures of our culture to have sex outside of marriage.

How to Strengthen Good Values

There are many other influences on your children. Some of those influences may not be good. When we stop to think of the time we get to spend with our children, it may be only a few minutes a day. That is all the time you have to make a direct influence on their lives. In the past children had helpful influence from other family members who lived close. Often that is no longer true. That is why we need to be sure the influences our children are under now will agree with our values.

Seek Pressure for Good from Other Young People

Do not think that just because your children are involved in a good group that they are under a good influence. Take the time to get to know the group leaders as well as the other young people in the group. You should know what influences your children are receiving and how to oppose any bad influence. It is also important that you talk to your children about what they are doing and about their friends. If you have a loving connection with them, you should know how things are going.

Get Involved with School and Teachers

Teachers are near the top of the list of people who influence young people. Parents should attend school meetings such as parent-teacher meetings. If there are any problems, call a teacher and ask for a meeting. Most teachers want to do a good job, but they may not share your Christian values.

Look carefully at what is in school books and classes. Although some teachers do not agree, parents are the ones most responsible for their children's education. Do not be afraid to object if you find offensive material in what your children are being taught.

Children Home Alone

If your young person is going to be home alone for several hours after school, who or what will influence him during that time? Will it be other young people, television or some other thing? Today the most common place for sex before marriage is at home in the afternoon when both parents are at work.

What can you do? You can try to get your child involved in something like sports or an after-school job. Or perhaps your child could go to the home of someone near where you live. Be sure that person is also a good example of what a Christian should be.

The Power of Books

It is important for you to understand that you can influence your children's thinking through good reading material. Try to develop in your children a love for good books, especially the Bible. Good books can serve to teach the Christian values you want your children to make their own. It is especially good to give your older children stories of great Christians of the past.

Directions for Helping Young People Use the Home Computer

Here are some helpful ideas to protect your children from bad influences on the computer.

- Establish rules for your children about computer use when they are away from home.
- Know about the issues of children's safety on the computer.

- Spend time on the computer beside each child and establish trust about computer use.
- Put your computer in an area of the home where you can easily watch your child.
- Daily ask your children about their computer friends and actions.
- Block personal messages from people you and your children do not know.
- Do not allow your children to put their pictures on-line because a bad person may see them.
- Discuss with your children what they can have on a free home page – no telephone number.
- Check with your children's school to see what is being put on school home pages.
- Check the amount of time your children spend on the computer and at what times of the day. Much time on the computer, especially at night, may show a problem.
- Watch for changes in your children's actions.[1]

Being a parent today is not easy. But with thought, planning and effort, we can give our children a healthy group of friends who share the Christian values we teach.

How to Teach God's Plan for Sex

The best place for young people to learn God's plan for sex is at home. Here are a few main elements about sex you should share with your children.

In the Beginning Was Sex

To understand sex in God's plan, we need to go back to the beginning. "Then the Lord God made man from the dust of the ground. And He breathed into his nose the breath of life. Man became a living being" (Genesis 2:7). Adam was the end of

God's plan for creation. "God saw all that He had made and it was very good" (Genesis 1:31).

Yet after the creation of man, God saw that something was not good. "Then the Lord God said, 'It is not good for man to be alone" (Genesis 2:18). God had "made man in His own likeness" (Genesis 1:27). This made man a social being because God is a social being. As good and perfect as God's creation was, it was not good that Adam was alone.

It is interesting that God did not solve Adam's problem of being alone by creating other men. Instead, he created woman. When woman appeared, God's creation was complete.

As you study God's plan for sex, three things become clear: (1) God is for sex; He created sex and wants us to enjoy it to the fullest. (2) The sex experience is meant to make a oneness between a man and a woman. (3) God designed sex for marriage.

God means for sex to be enjoyable for a husband and a wife. You can see that clearly in Proverbs 5:18-19: "Let your well be honored, and be happy with the wife you married when you were young. Let her be like a loving female deer. Let her breasts please you at all times. Be filled with great joy always because of her love."

Eve was not only a friend for Adam, but her coming made possible a special kind of oneness in every way. "For this reason a man will leave his father and his mother, and will be joined to his wife and they will become one flesh" (Genesis 2:24). That means more than just the bodies. It also includes the mind and the soul.

In God's plan marriage is the permanent uniting of two people. Paul used the example of Christ and the church to provide a deeper understanding of that uniting (Ephesians 5:31-32). Based on that relationship, a Christian husband and a Christian wife do not divorce. This Christian way is very different from a culture where people divorce for the smallest reasons.

God's Plan for Sex

It helps young people say no to sex if they understand that God has an exact plan for their sex life. There are three main reasons for sex in marriage: to develop oneness between husband and wife, to have children, and for enjoyment. One young person said it well: "Rules, and especially God's rules, are good teaching that give greater peace and joy in our lives than we could ever imagine."

How to Teach About Sex at Home

One young person wrote to me:

> Parents need to be more active in developing their child's understanding of sex. The parents should offer guidance and point the child in the right direction. Letting a child get into a situation that he or she is not able to deal with can easily lead to damage. In young people the mind is often not as developed as the body. Parents need to be involved in each part of the child's changing sexuality. It is never too late to start teaching your children about sex.

Where to Begin

We need to let our children know that the body is a wonderful gift from God. They need to know that all body parts and works are normal and that we do not need to be ashamed of them. Real discussion and teaching about sex needs to begin as early as three or four years of age. The only thing to be decided is if our children will learn from us or from our culture.

The younger children are, the more they want their parents to teach them about life and everything in it. Keep in mind that it is always more difficult to correct wrong thinking than to keep a child from learning it. If we begin early to teach our children, we can save both us and them much sorrow later.

What to Say

Teach your children things they can understand at their age. Be guided by the questions they ask. Teaching a child too much too soon can cause misunderstanding and fear. When you talk about sex, use the correct words. That way they will know when the wrong words are used by others. If you do not know all you should know, get the facts from a book or from your family doctor.

As your children grow older, teach them about the results of their words and actions in the area of sex. Next, teach your children that their nature is shown by what they say and do. It shows their opinion about sex. Always teach about sex with values included. What we do sexually involves our relationship with God. He knows and wants only what is best for us.

How to Say It

Your children will ask many questions. Use those questions to teach. If you and your child see a pregnant woman, talk about that. You can share God's purpose for sex and its beauty. Talk about how people today are very distant from God's creative design. Know how well your child can understand and the level of his interest.

How to Teach Christian Values About Sex

Teaching the Christian position on relationships to our children is one of the most important things we can do for them. It will help them to say no to sex before marriage. Let us consider four ways the Christian position should be different from the world's position.

First, the Christian believes that each person is special and of great worth because each one is made in the likeness of God. Each one is worthy of consideration.

Second, the Christian believes that we should not use people to meet our own needs.

Third, the Christian believes that we should treat others with the love and respect God gives us. First Corinthians 13:4-8 tells how God loves us. That is the kind of love we want to receive from other people. So it is the kind of love we must have for them (Matthew 7:12).

Fourth, the Christian believes in the value of waiting. "Love does not give up," 1 Corinthians 13:4 says. The marriage bed is the time and place for sexual closeness and enjoyment.

How can you teach biblical values about sex to your young people? The first and most important way is by example. Actions speak louder than words. But there is a need for planned teaching as well. This kind of teaching takes place most easily at times such as when the family is eating together. But whenever you teach, you have to plan for it.

Younger children will enjoy spending this kind of time with you. But older children may find it more difficult. It may seem hard when you first try to do it. Stay with it. You and your children will get used to it and end up having some great times together. Sex needs to be discussed in the home. Children need to understand that sex is so wonderful that it is worth waiting for. Our goal as parents is not to keep sex unknown, just unexplored.

Chapter 19
Help Children Develop the Strength to Say No

"Alyson, I really love you."

"I love you too, Brett."

"Then we should celebrate."

"Celebrate? What do you mean?"

"You know, the way most people celebrate when they are deeply in love."

"Are you talking about sex? Brett, I love you. I really do. But love does not mean sex to me yet. I have decided to remain untouched until I get married – until we get married, if we ever do."

"Love means sex! Sex means love!"

"No, Brett, I will not have sex until I am married. If you cannot wait until then, maybe you are not the one I am waiting for."

"But Alyson – can we talk about this?"

"No. I made up my mind two years ago. I feel deeply about you, but the answer is no."

Where does the strength to say no to sex come from, even when it may be something a young person wants? It begins with developing firm beliefs and a conscience about sex.

Help Your Children Form Strong Beliefs

A person without strong beliefs will usually follow the leader of any group he happens to be with. But someone who can stand up and say, "I have my reasons," will usually have the strength to do right even if he does it alone. Consider what this young person shared with me about strong beliefs: "It is hard to wait, to be self-controlled, when all the others are 'doing it.' But firm beliefs are great things for any of us to have."

The Word of God is our only base for strong beliefs. The Bible is clear:

> Have nothing to do with sex sins! Any other sin that a man does, does not hurt his own body. But the man who does a sex sin sins against his own body. Do you know that your body is a house of God where the Holy Spirit lives? God gave you His Holy Spirit. Now you belong to God. You do not belong to yourselves. God bought you with a great price. So honor God with your body. You belong to Him. (1 Corinthians 6:18-20)

> God wants you to be holy. You must keep away from sex sins. God wants each of you to use his body in the right way by keeping it holy and by respecting it. You should not use it to please your own desires like the people who do not know God. (1 Thessalonians 4:3-5)

Young people need a completely Christian way of looking at the world. That will affect how they act, including their sexual relationships. But most young people today do not see the world as based on God's truth.

A Need for Change

Children learn to copy the world that they see around them. They form their thoughts on what they see others doing. The

173

Bible says, "Do not act like the sinful people of the world" (Romans 12:2).

Beliefs are formed as children watch their parents and hear why they act as they do. That is why God gave us the family – to be the environment in which children learn and develop their own beliefs about love, sex and marriage. But many parents today have no strong beliefs about sexual values. That makes it difficult for a child to develop any personal beliefs, especially in an area as inviting as sex.

Because of this, a change is necessary for both the children and their parents. Romans 12:2 continues, "Let God change your life . . . . let Him give you a new mind." That change involves three important facts. First, we need to teach what the Bible says about sex. Second, we need the Holy Spirit to make the change. Third, we need to act in a way that shows the beliefs we want our young people to develop.

Sometimes we work with children from homes where the family has failed. Then the church must try to provide a way in which God can change their minds. We must be like a family to them. It is not enough just to talk, even if our words are biblical. Only in loving relationships can truth be made a living part of one's life.

Changed by God's Truth

Young people need to know the whole truth, not just the truth about sex. They need to know that they are created in God's likeness. That is what makes them able to have a relationship with God and with people. They need to know that they have value and worth because God gave His Son to die for them. They need to know that God loves them with unconditional love and wants to have a relationship with them. They need to know that being loved and accepted by God is the base for their own security. They need to know that the way to show their love for God is to serve others.

Understanding these truths is the Christian's base for all actions and relationships, including sexual relationships. A young person with Christian beliefs will have a much easier time controlling himself. That is because he is driven by true love instead of by sexual desire. Remember, sexual desire cannot wait to get, while true love cannot wait to give. A young person's beliefs must be deep within him. Only then will those beliefs be respected by others.

The Holy Spirit plays an important part in changing our minds. Some of the fruits of the Spirit are self-control, gentleness, kindness and goodness. When Jesus called His disciples, He simply said, "Follow me." Then, through their loving relationship with Him, they grew in their understanding of the teachings and truths of the faith.

When you help your children develop their beliefs by providing directions for their actions, you help them in three important ways: First, they have a way out. Caught in a hard situation, the young person can always say, "I am sorry, my parents will not let me."

Second, they will know how to decide. Tell young people, "You can do whatever you want within these limits." Then they have fewer things they can choose from and it is easier for them to decide. They will be more sure why they decided that way and more able to do what they decided.

Third, they can show self-control. When young people follow directions, they learn to obey. When they learn to obey, they learn self-control. Young people must understand that they are going to run into conflict with their friends as they develop and act on their own beliefs. But by developing strong personal beliefs, they will respect themselves and feel complete.

Help Your Children Form a Christian Conscience

Our conscience reminds us to do the right thing. If we see the world by God's rules, our conscience will show that. If we see the world without God, our conscience will not be able to give us good guidance.

Many things help to form our conscience – the people we like and spend time with, the ideas we consider, the media we see and hear. One young person wrote about how she learned to silence her conscience:

> I was raised in a good Christian home. I was always taught that sex before marriage was wrong. When my boyfriend and I began to get involved sexually, I felt guilty at first. Before long, though, I could not understand why I ever felt bad about having sex.

If I, as a Christian, listen to my conscience, I can sense the Holy Spirit's voice as He seeks to guide my actions. Ask your young people to consider these four questions to see how they are forming their consciences:

- Are you doing things now that you once said you would never do?
- Did you ever look down on others for doing what you are now doing?
- Are you doing things now, without feeling guilt, that once troubled you?
- Have you allowed a boyfriend or a girlfriend to silence your conscience about getting more and more involved in sex?

If the answer to any of these is yes, your child's conscience needs to be reformed. How can you do that? Here are some simple ideas you can use to help your child develop a working Christian conscience:

- Ask the Holy Spirit to help you clean and reform your conscience.
- Fill your mind with God's rules about life, love and values.
- Limit your relationships to real Christians who already have a Christian conscience.

Urge Your Child to Promise Not to Have Sex

Not having sex is the only safe sex. So urging our children to promise not to do it until marriage is well worth the effort. A study shows that sex education in school has not worked. In fact, children who have had sex education in school are more likely to have sex than those who have not. But the not-doing-it message seems to be having good effects.[1]

Each year there are more and more young people signing up for programs such as the True Love Waits program. Making the promise to wait has helped hundreds of thousands of young people wait for sex until marriage. A study reported in *The Journal of the American Medical Association* in 1997 found that 16 percent of girls and 10 percent of boys had made the promise to wait.

The Kaiser Family Foundation found that "the more importance young people place on religion, the more likely they are to say that religion is their reason for delaying sex." Without a biblical way of looking at life, children feel unsure and empty. This leaves them powerless to oppose sexual pressures. Without guidance, children do not know right and wrong. They know only that they have found a closeness that makes them feel good for a short time.

How Far Is Too Far?

We need to be prepared to answer a difficult question: How far can I go? Or even better, how far should I go? The Bible does not give exact answers in every area of sex. But it does give some clear directions for escaping sex sin.

Everything But

True godliness results not only in obeying the letter of the law but also in obeying the spirit of the law. Doing "everything but--" certainly disobeys the spirit of God's command to "have nothing to do with sex sins!" If we truly want to please God, we cannot base our sexual limits on "everything but--."

On the Edge of Sexual Danger

While some do not want to go too far, they want to go as far as possible. That is because they are afraid they might miss out on something exciting. Most people who do that end up disobeying both the spirit of the law and the letter of the law. Most young people think they can stop before it goes too far. However, this is not how we are made. Once sexual excitement begins it is not our nature to stop short of full satisfaction. When it comes to sex before marriage, that is too far.

Measuring How Far

How far is too far? Explaining how believers can live a God-pleasing life, Paul wrote:

> God wants you to be holy. You must keep away from sex sins. God wants each of you to use his body in the right way by keeping it holy and by respecting it. You should not use it to please your own desires like the people who do not know God. No man should do wrong to his Christian brother in anything. The Lord will

punish a person who does. I have told you this before (1 Thessalonians 4:3-6).

You have sinned against a brother when you have excited him to the point where that excitement cannot be satisfied in a way that would be pleasing to God. Some excitement in a boy-girl relationship is normal and should not be a concern. But if it becomes so strong that it controls actions, then it is sin. To keep from sinning against another person, each person must decide the point at which the other will lose control. Then that point must become a personal limit.

Limited Freedom?

Once you are sexually excited, you begin to limit your freedom to say no. Many situations rob young people of their freedom to say no. First, situations such as certain kinds of music and activities can excite sexual desires. Young people should be warned about the danger of these things.

Second, kissing and touching prepares the body for sexual action. The pleasing feelings that come from touching certain areas of the body can cause a person to lose control.

Third, drugs and drinking affect the mind. They give a false sense of security and well-being. Then the brain is not able to choose wisely and wait for sex.

Reasonable Advice for Drawing the Line

Instead of asking how far one can go, it is best to stay away from dangerous situations completely. How do young people set their limits? Here is a good example given by a student:

> My advice: no long periods of kissing. No lying down while kissing. No feeling the other person's body. No clothing that shows too much of the body. I would also

advise spending time in groups instead of alone. Plan so that there will not be much free time to get into trouble.

When young people are thinking about where to set their limits, questions like these are helpful:

- Do I really want to honor and serve the Lord?
- How far would I go if I could see that Jesus was in the room?
- Will my actions help my friend and me grow closer to Christ?
- Is this action making the temptation for more physical involvement greater?
- Am I really as serious about this person as my actions express?
- If we separate, will we still be able to think well of each other?

Ways for Keeping Sexual Rules

Talk, the way we move our bodies and even the clothes we wear are ways of saying no to sexual sin. The secret is for a young person to have security in himself. If young people know who they are in Christ, they can stand with their friends and say no to sex before marriage.

Keep the Mind Pure

Scripture tells us to "take hold of every thought and make it obey Christ" (2 Corinthians 10:5). We may not have much control over thoughts that come into our minds, but we can decide not to let them stay there. Here are three steps we can take to keep a pure mind: First, we need to know the nature of God. He is holy, pure, truthful, just and loving. Second, we need to discover the will of God from the study of the Scriptures and from listening to godly people. Third, we need to keep ourselves in a godly environment and seek the help and advice of godly people.

Remember that God always gives us the strength to do what He commands. In Philippians 4:8 Paul says, "Christian brothers, keep your minds thinking about whatever is true, whatever is respected, whatever is right, whatever is pure, whatever can be loved, and whatever is well thought of. If there is anything good and worth giving thanks for, think about these things."

Urge your young people to be careful about what they watch, read and hear. Once a picture is formed in their minds, it is there to stay. So be careful about what you let in. The more we have accepted the world's values, the harder it is to form our minds to the thoughts, ideas and values of God.

Glorify God with Your Body

In 1 Timothy 2:9 Paul said, "Christian women should not be dressed in the kind of clothes and their hair should not be combed in a way that will make people look at them." A girl may not understand that a boy does not think of her clothes the way she does. Boys are excited by what they see. Since girls are excited more by touch, many of them do not understand this. This is an area where parents, especially mothers, need to educate their girls to understand the effect their clothes can have on men.

Christian men and women do not have to deny being men and women. But they do have to use their bodies in a way that is glorifying to God and will not cause others to sin. One girl gave this excellent advice: "On a date (really, all the time), wear clothes that you would want to meet Jesus in. They can be nice looking but not designed to excite men."

Choose Friends Carefully

Paul knew about the great pressure friends put on friends. In 1 Corinthians 5:9 he said, "I told you in my letter not to keep on being with people who do any kind of sex sins." The pressure friends put on friends can be either good or bad. As one student said: "I know that my friends have a great influence on who I am and on what my values are. Godly friends can be a real help when having problems with sexual desires."

The issue for young people comes down to choosing friends carefully. They should not spend much time with friends who do not share their values and beliefs. They should choose to be with friends who do share their values and beliefs.

We live in a world where it seems as if everyone is saying yes to sex before marriage. That is why it is very important for young people to join with others who are saying no. The strength they draw from friends can help young people face sexual pressure.

Seek Close Relationships but Not Too Close

Spending too much time together almost always causes sexual problems for two young people. When a boy and a girl spend all their time together, the temptation becomes too strong. I advise that young people spend most of their time together in groups until they are older and seriously want to find a person to marry.

Seek the Wisdom of Others

In seeking advice, young people need to search for people of godly understanding, Christians who know them and care about them. In addition to parents, young people can look to people such as pastors, young people's leaders and Sunday school teachers. Young people need to seek advice, not just confirmation. To seek confirmation means to go to someone who will agree with you about what you have already decided. To seek advice means to go to someone and ask for guidance.

Ask God to Help

Most young people who have developed strong beliefs about dealing with sexual pressures know they need to ask God for help. Nothing in this book will be effective if young people do not understand their need for God's help. This young person agrees:

> Although it may seem that your sexual desires cannot be controlled, there is one sure way to help you hold back: Give your life completely to Jesus Christ. Ask Him to come into your heart and be the Lord of every part of your life, including your sexual nature and desires.

When young people see their need for help in dealing with their sexuality, they are very open to Christ's invitation to a personal relationship. We must urge our young people to use prayer as the first step to a sexual life that honors God. We also must urge young people to go beyond a "please help me" relationship with God. Their goal should be to learn and follow His will in all things. The deeper their relationship becomes with the heavenly Father, the more help they will receive for living a Christian life.

Chapter 20
Help Young People Set Limits for Dating

We must help young people decide how they will act in a dating relationship. A student wrote about the importance of rules for dating: "Set your rules now, not when you are deep into a relationship. Set them by what is right in the eyes of God."

Christian young people should decide how far they will go on a date. It is best if this is done long before they come close to being involved in any sexual situation. What are some rules for setting sexual limits? How do Christian young people "draw the line"? Here is an example:

> I have promised not to have any kind of physical relationship with a man before I am married, not even kissing. That surprises people because sex is taken so lightly these days and kissing is just for fun. But how can I think pure thoughts when I am pressed close to a man's body? How can I set my mind on "things in heaven" (Colossians 3:2) when someone's mouth is pressed on mine?

Here is the rule I used before I married: I will treat a woman on a date the same way I want some other man to treat the woman I will marry some day.

It is good for young people to share their limits with the person they date. That clears the air to discuss dating limits. If a young woman does not let her date know her limits, she must be prepared for him to be angry when she stops him from breaking one of her rules. When the other person knows what the limits are, it is easier for both of them to remember.

How to Keep Control When Dating

Here are a number of useful ways for helping young people control sexual drives and temptations in a dating relationship.[1]

Date Only Those with the Same Beliefs as Yours

One of the main rules for dating relationships is that a Christian should not date a non-Christian. Second Corinthians 6:14 is clear, "Do not be joined together with those who do not belong to Christ."

A Christian dating a non-Christian is dangerous for at least two reasons. First, everyone a person dates is a possible candidate for marriage. Second, a non-Christian does not share a Christian's beliefs. The people your children date should be Christians, but not all Christians understand God's rules for living in the same way. The people your children date should accept the same rules for living the Christian life as your family does.

Young people seem to think about three things when considering a person to date: looks, how much fun they are, and how popular they are. But these do not say much about the person.

This young woman's story shows the importance of young people dating only people who share their beliefs about sexual purity:

> At 24, I am eight months pregnant and unmarried. That has forced me to decide many things I never thought I would have to decide. It has greatly changed my life.
>
> Perhaps the biggest surprise is that I am a born-again Christian. How did this happen? It all started when I chose to date a non-Christian. I was honest with my boyfriend about the importance of my relationship with

Jesus. Rick knew that I believed sex was for marriage. He did not agree with me, but he did not push me.

Two times in the eight months before I got pregnant I told him I thought we should end our relationship. I knew 2 Corinthians 6:14 says, "Do not be joined together with those who do not belong to Christ." But Rick would say, "Just because I do not have the same beliefs does not mean we do not have great times together."

To me, Christianity was not just a belief. It was a way of life. Still, what he said seemed to be true enough. Once when I said I would never marry a non-Christian, he said he did not want to get married but he did want to date me.

Without ever meaning to, I was slowly falling in love. I felt the freedom to be myself when I was with Rick. That was not true when I had dated a Christian who expected nothing less than perfection. My relationship with Rick was a cheerful one.

Without wanting to admit it, it was the beginning of compromise. People did not see that I was leaving God behind. I was still busy in our church and enjoyed it. But the more interested I became in Rick, the easier it was to let my guard down. A good-night kiss during our first month of dating turned into hours of exciting kissing later. I started to excuse staying at his house all night because of the half-hour drive home.

By the time we had sex, it was so easy to give in. I knew that dating Rick was not God's will for me. At first I excused it because the relationship was not important to me. Then, when I could not use that excuse, I just did not care. At that point I was not afraid of sinning.

I had to decide many hard things after I became pregnant. Most important, I needed to get right with God again. I needed forgiveness. I also needed to become firm in the Word. I decided to leave everything. I moved a distance away to live with friends. They love the Lord and have become like family to me. I also learned that an unwanted pregnancy is not the same as an unwanted child. I decided to give the child up for adoption.

God tells us to wait. That is because He loves us and knows what is best for us. Over the past several months, I have been dealing with my sin. I have also seen the goodness of God as never before. Ephesians 1:7-8 has become so real to me: "Because of the blood of Christ, we are bought and made free from the punishment of sin. And because of His blood, our sins are forgiven. His loving-favor to us is so rich." I chose to go God's way.

If you really want to control the sexual area of your life, be careful about the way you live. Be careful about the way those you date live. Date only those who believe the way you do, and be responsible to each other.

Set Dating Goals

A recent study of dating among young people showed that "by age 17, the sex act is an accepted, if not an expected, part of dating relationships."[2] For that and other reasons, it is important for young people to have goals for their dating relationships. Here are some possible dating goals:

- Be accepting of the other person by honoring his or her God-given station in life.
- Build up the other person by showing honor for the things that person can do.
- Help fulfill the other person's goals.

- Be responsible to the other person for fulfilling your own goals.
- In every situation, try to show Jesus Christ in your spirit and actions.

Make Clear Plans for Each Date

Plan your dating carefully. Here is some advice from young people who are learning to plan a date:

> We found we needed to do things with other unmarried people. It was so nice to spend a quiet evening at home, but all too often it was easy to get carried away.

* * * * *

> Do not leave the plan of what you will do or where you will go on a date. Changes of plans usually mean trouble.

* * * * *

> Do not listen to bad music or see bad motion pictures. That only makes you want to act out what you have seen or heard.

A date should always provide time for talking, since that is the best way to get to know someone. This is especially true of a first date. That gives you a chance to explore common interests. Planning should be seen as a way to stay away from sexual involvement. It will also bring about growth in both of you.

Talk Openly About Sex

A young person who does not talk openly about his beliefs about sex may get into trouble. Here is what a student wrote: "Make your limits known to each other. Be honest when you see a problem coming. If you are honest, your friend will begin to feel good about sharing as well."

Include Prayer

Here is a prayer one student prays before each date: "Dear Lord, Trusting You for strength, I promise to keep myself pure for the person I am to marry by staying away from sex and from any other physical expressions that do not honor You." Such a prayer, prayed before each date, could certainly help to keep a person's dating life on the right road. Here are some things to remember about praying together on a date:

- Be short. Prayer can be very personal. The closeness developed in praying together can easily lead to closeness on a sexual level.
- Pray for the needs of others.
- Be careful about touching when praying.
- Do not pray about feeling bad about your sexual problems. Do that when you are alone.

Try Not to Be Alone Together

Many times being alone together is more than young people can control. The way for young people to take care of that kind of temptation is not to put themselves in it.

Parents can help. Do not be afraid to ask your children where they are going, what their plans are and when they will be back. Set reasonable limits and let them know what you expect from them in their dating. By holding them responsible, you also provide them with clear answers to pressures from their dating friends. When pressured they can simply answer, "My parents do not allow me to have friends over when they are not home."

Stop Thinking of the Body and Work at Building the Relationship

Young people who want godly relationships need to put away the sex part and look to building the other parts of their relationship. One young person wrote:

> When you begin to develop a relationship, try to start out as friends. You usually do not want to hurt a friend. Even more, you would likely see this person in a spiritual way. This is important. Two people need to know each other spiritually so that later they can deal with problems in the right way.

Another young woman says that leaving sex out of the relationship can bring about several good things:

1. Keeping yourselves from sex will give you something to look forward to in marriage.
2. A promise to not have sex will please the Lord and will take away much guilt you may have.
3. It will help you discover new areas in each other you have not yet examined.

Give Your Children Ways to Escape

We need to give our children ways to get out of a bad situation. Here are several "escape paths" I give young people.

Make a Promise to be Faithful to God

Help your children use bad situations to confirm their promise to obey God and keep Him first in their relationships. One young woman wrote me about this:

> I knew what I had to do. I had to give Ken back to the Lord and put Jesus first. Jesus should have been first all

along. I was so afraid. For over a year I had been holding on to Ken. I dreamed that one day I would become more to Ken than just for sex. Still how could I become more to Ken when I had let myself become so much less?

However much we love another person, Jesus must always be our first love. When He is the center of our lives, all other things will fall into their correct places. If God is no longer first in a young person's life, the first escape path from a bad situation is to give his life back to God. One young man advises:

> Give God a chance to work in your relationship. Promise Him that you will stop being sexually involved and that you will wait for the right time and the right person. If you and your girlfriend really are in love, your love for each other will grow deeper as you build your relationship on the Lord and save sex for marriage.

Getting Out of a Relationship

Do you remember Pat? We gave her story in chapter 5. Pat first had sex when she was 16. She became a Christian the next year. Later she learned that sex outside marriage is wrong. She felt bad that she could not break her sex habit. Finally, Pat stopped dating for about two years so that she could get her thoughts together. That was a time of great spiritual growth for her.

Backing away from ungodly dating relationships is very difficult. One girl gives this advice to her friends:

> If you have already had sex, do not think that the Lord is through with you. If you have sinned, you need to ask the Lord's forgiveness, but you also need to forgive yourself. Although you cannot change the past, if the Lord has forgiven you, there is nothing to do but forget it and go forward. By forward, I mean end your sinful relationship.

Romans 8:28 promises, "We know that God makes all things work together for the good of those who love Him and are chosen to be a part of His plan." That's a good promise from God. Do not let Satan continue to trip you up with sin. Ephesians 3:20 says, "God is able to do much more than we ask or think through His power working in us." Give Him that chance.

Look for a Way to Get Out

The Bible is clear about temptation:

> You have never been tempted to sin in any different way than other people. God is faithful. He will not allow you to be tempted more than you can take. But when you are tempted, He will make a way for you to keep from falling into sin. (1 Corinthians 10:13)

Young people must understand that they have a way to get out of any situation. It is the power to say no. God will always give us strength equal to the temptation. The best way out is to escape before the bad situation develops. The most effective way is to just say no.

Get Out Fast

I often tell young people, "If you cannot take care of the situation, get out of there. Run as fast as you can!" That is the message of several Scriptures. First Corinthians 6:18 teaches, "Have nothing to do with sex sins!" Second Timothy 2:22 says, "Turn away from the sinful things young people want to do." James 4:7 tells us: "So give yourselves to God. Stand against the devil and he will run away from you."

Chapter 21

Forgive and Provide Hope When Children Sin

Our culture tells our young people, "If it feels good, do it." But sexual guilt among young people is increasing. So many young people want to be forgiven. Here are the words of just one of them:

> I had sex with my boyfriend thinking I owed it to him. When I told him I was pregnant, he got angry and blamed me. He said I should have the baby killed before it was born. So, to save my parents sorrow and to keep Matt, I did what he said. Now Matt has left me. How can God love me after all I have done? Can God really love and forgive me?

We need to understand that people with sexual guilt may find it very hard to accept the idea of forgiveness. There are many Christian young people who have asked for God's forgiveness, and they are forgiven. Yet they go through life without the joy that comes from forgiveness.

The Gift of Forgiveness

Especially for parents, acceptance begins with forgiveness. Be forgiving. Here are three helpful guidelines:

First, begin. God's love commands us to begin by offering forgiveness. "But God showed His love to us. While we were still sinners, Christ died for us" (Romans 5:8). He took the first step – paying the price by dying for our sins. Then He offered us His forgiveness. As God's children, we must follow our heavenly Father's example and begin by forgiving.

Second, try to fix the relationship. So often when young people become involved in sex, the relationship with their parents is broken. God wants parents to take responsibility for their part in a broken relationship and to begin rebuilding it. If we do not, God does not want our worship. Jesus said, "If you take your gift to the altar and remember your brother [son, daughter] has something against you, leave your gift on the altar. Go and make right what is wrong between you and him. Then come back and give your gift" (Matthew 5:23-24).

Third, be truly forgiving. Forgiveness knows that a wrong has been done but accepts it and forgets it. God said He puts all our sins behind Him. He has buried them in the deepest sea. That is what God does when He forgives us. We must do the same when we forgive our young people.

A Picture of God's Forgiveness

Young people usually see God through parents and church leaders. If we are forgiving, it is easier for our children to see God as forgiving. The actions and words of parents can stand in the way of their children ever accepting God's forgiveness. For example, several years ago I talked with a young woman. She had had a hard time experiencing God's forgiveness because of her relationship with her parents, especially her father. Tracy explains:

> My mother drank and was never really there for me. I was the youngest of five children and my sister Donna became a mother to me. Though I had no relationship with my father, I still tried to show him my love. I was so afraid of him, but I still wanted him to take an interest in me.
>
> As I grew up, I was always getting sick or hurt in order to get my parents to show some concern for me. Most of the time Donna was not blamed for the things she did. She was always being bad, getting into drugs and other

things. But my parents believed everything she said. They always said to me, "Tracy, you are lying to us." I was not lying. That was very hard to understand.

At 14, Tracy had her first sexual experience. She was not sexually involved again until she was 16, when she became pregnant. Her mother, who had recently accepted Christ, and her unbelieving father demanded that she have the baby killed before birth. After that, Tracy cried for three months. She hated her parents and felt so hurt and alone.

Several months later her father accepted Christ. After watching the spiritual growth of her parents, Tracy invited Christ into her life. For the next two years she grew as a Christian. Then she went to a Christian college and began to speak out against killing unborn babies. After she told her own story, she felt that other Christians were judging her. That hurt her Christian walk.

Tracy began dating a Christian man, and soon he asked her to marry him. He started asking her to have sex with him, but she refused. Finally one night he forced her. That was a terrible experience for her. Over the next three years, Tracy had relationships with seven different men. In most cases, sex ended the relationship.

> I began to think, these are Christian men but they do not think much of me. If they did they would not demand to have sex. They think I am nothing, that I have no worth or value. Maybe they are right.

> I decided I might as well go back to being what I used to be. First I had sex with a man who was not a Christian. I knew it was wrong. I did not really want to do it. Everybody who did not know my life story thought I was a wonderful person. I still read the Bible and took part in church.

Having Christians condemn me, though, made me stop being so much involved with church. I began to date a really nice man. When his parents found out about my dead baby, they made him stop dating me. That really hurt. I decided I would find a man who looked like him, sleep with him and become pregnant. Then people would blame it on the man who had hurt me so much. I would not say it was his child, but it would look like him. I did that and became pregnant, but the baby died before it was born.

Tracy cried much the next two years. She was ready to give up on God when she met Dave, another Christian. After a month of dating, they planned to marry. When they became sexually involved, Tracy fell apart. She broke off their relationship.

I started to think about killing myself. But the day I was preparing to do it, I thought of my family. I began to think I must not do this because the children of my brother and sister would grow up thinking that Christianity does not work. At that minute the telephone rang. It was my older brother. He knew nothing of what was going on in my life. He said, "Tracy, you are thinking of taking your life, right? You are thinking you have no hope." I could not believe it. This was my brother who had left home when I was 8 years old and I had never really known him.

I said, "Wait a minute; are you serious?" He told me that he and his wife had been praying just minutes before. God had shown them exactly what I was going through. Then I knew God is real and could change me. I had begged Him for years, but I still was missing something. I did not understand what it was.

Like so many people, Tracy's idea of God was very much affected by her relationship with her father. To her, God was a dictator, unforgiving and distant. Without a change in her idea of God, she would never be free to understand and accept His forgiveness. Her idea of God began to change when she began talking with my friend Dick Day, a Christian adviser.

> I listened to Dick Day talking about repentance and changing my thinking about God. I began to understand who God is. He loved me and wanted me and He paid for my sins. I had heard those things before. Now I finally began to understand them. I learned about God's nature. He is holy. Holiness cannot exist with sin. I understood that because of Jesus' death, God's judgment was satisfied where I was concerned. It was so good to know that God loves me and gave His Son so that I could be forgiven and made clean.
>
> I began to see my worth and value to God. He made me who I am and how I am. God did not need me, but because of His love He wanted me. Because He wanted me, He provided a way for me to repent, confess my sins and know that they are forgiven.
>
> Finally I understood that God wanted to cover my sins and make me new. That gave me a whole new way of thinking. From that time I had new ideas about prayer, about God and about myself.

When Dick first met Tracy, she was full of worry and hated everything. Three months later she was a happy Christian. Because she then saw herself differently, Tracy was also beginning to see other people differently. She was even beginning to see her father differently.

> Over the years since my father became a Christian, he has been changing. I had this idea of my father because of the past. So when he was changing, I could not scc it.

Forgiven and clean, Tracy had become free to begin a new relationship with Dave. For both of them, that was a new beginning.

> Before that, we did not really have a relationship. We knew each other some, but sex had just taken over. After understanding God's nature, we came back together. It was completely different. Then Dave and I had the freedom to talk and understand who each of us really was. We again made plans to get married. Until then, I could not trust either God or Dave. The other times I had planned to marry, I could not really promise my whole self. I could just promise my body.

After experiencing such hard times in relating to men, Tracy was now free to commit herself in marriage. She and Dave were married, and their relationship is growing. It is based on an understanding of who God is and what love and forgiveness are all about. The love and acceptance given her by other Christians helped. They did not just talk about God's love, acceptance and forgiveness. They lived it.

What the Bible Says About Forgiveness

First, let us consider an important person in the Old Testament, David. He was the king. When he saw Bathsheba, David did not just look at her. He watched her. The minute he begin to watch, he was caught. After learning that her husband, Uriah, was away in the army, David sent for Bathsheba. Sometime later she sent word to him that she was pregnant.

David knew he was in trouble. He sent for Uriah, hoping that while he was home he would sleep with his wife. David's plan did not work. Uriah slept in the servants' part of the palace. David even tried to talk Uriah into going home to his wife and "enjoying himself." But he refused, unwilling to leave his men.

David did not give up. He got Uriah drunk, hoping he would go make love to his wife.

When none of that worked, David ordered Uriah sent to the front of the battle, where he was killed. Now look at what happened next. David admitted his sin and asked God to forgive him: "I have done what is sinful in Your eyes. You are always right when You speak, and fair when You judge. . . . Take away my sin, and I will be clean. Wash me, and I will be whiter than snow" (Psalm 51:4, 7).

Here was a man who had had sex with another man's wife and then killed the husband. But is there any sin so terrible that God cannot forgive it? The answer is no, not even sexual sin, not even murder. There are five steps to God's forgiveness:

First, admit your sin. First John 1:9 tells us we must confess our sin. To confess means to tell God you agree with Him about your sin.

Second, accept God's forgiveness. Colossians 2:13 says, "God forgave your sins and gave you new life through Christ." Some people are sure that God could never forgive them because they have sinned too much. The Good News is that Jesus did not come to save good people. He came to save sinners. He said, "I have not come to call good people. I have come to call sinners to be sorry for their sins and to turn from them" (Luke 5:32).

Third, show you have repented. God says, "Do something to show me that your hearts are changed" (Matthew 3:8). Repentance means turning around, changing one's mind. Ask God how you should show it. It might be by ending a relationship. It might mean changing your way of living.

Fourth, forgive yourself. When we refuse to forgive ourselves, we really are rejecting God's loving grace. If God's grace cannot cover the sin in your life, it cannot cover any sin.

Fifth, do not let Satan lead you wrong. Satan will try to make you feel condemned. But Romans 8:1 says, "Those who belong to Christ will not suffer the punishment of sin." So, if you have sinned, admit your sin to God, repent, accept God's forgiveness and forgive yourself. Do not let Satan rob you of the joy of God's forgiveness.

What Can Be Done About Lost Purity?

No one can regain lost purity of the body. Once it is lost, it is gone forever. But one's spiritual purity can be regained. Romans 12:2 says, "Let God change your life. First of all, let Him give you a new mind." To give you a new mind, God has given three things. First, He has given His truth – to understand Who He is and who we are. Second, He has given His Holy Spirit – to show His truth and to bring it into our lives. Third, He has given His people – to express His love and forgiveness in relationships.

Young people who are sexually involved need a new beginning. The problem is that sexual sin can cause a person to take his eyes off Christ's love and forgiveness. He begins to lose all hope of living a pure life. But we do not have to feel trapped into continuing down a wrong path.

A young person just married wrote to me:

> My boyfriend and I knew we had to get out of our sexual sin. With God's help we did not have sex during the last nine months before we were married. The first time we made love after our marriage, tears of joy came down my face. I experienced the true beauty of the sexual relationship as God meant it to be.

Hope Lives On

For the young person who is under the pain of sexual sin, I can think of no more hopeful words than those of Dr. John Diggs:

> Hope lives on. Whatever mistakes you have made can be left in the past. How you have acted can be changed. If you have been involved in sexual sin, you can stop. If you have an STD, you can get treatment. If you have had a child before marriage, you can make sure it never happens again. If you have had your baby killed, you can keep from making that mistake in the future. You can find healing for your deep hurt.

Glossary

(This glossary gives the meaning for words as they are used in this book. Some words have more than one meaning. Look in a dictionary for the full meaning.)

abortion (a-BOR-shun): the removing and killing of a child before he or she is born

abstinence (AB-sta-nunce): doing without something, especially saving sex for marriage

adult (a-DULT): a man or woman who is fully grown up

adultery (a-DUL-ter-ee): having sex with anyone other than one's husband or wife

AIDS: a condition that makes a person more likely to develop serious health problems leading to death, gotten mainly through an STD called HIV

alcohol (AL-ca-hall): the element in wine and other strong drinks that makes people do things they would not otherwise do

amaze (a-MAZE): surprise, wonder

breast cancer (breast CAN-sir): cancer in the top, front part of a woman's body

cervical cancer (SIR-ve-cal CAN-sir): cancer in a part of the woman's reproductive members

chlamydia (cla-MID-ee-a): an STD that is much like gonorrhea

condom (CON-dum): a sleeve that fits over the male sex member to keep the woman from becoming pregnant or getting an STD

date: a set time to be with a person of the opposite sex

divorce (de-VORCE): the legal ending of a marriage

education (ed-u-KAY-shun): a program to learn things and develop the mind

genital (JEN-a-tul): the sex parts of the body

genital herpes (JEN-a-tul HER-pez): herpes is a disease that causes many small wounds in different parts of the body; genital herpes is herpes of the sex members

gonorrhea (GON-a-REE-a): one of the most common STDs.

grandchild (GRAND-child): a child of a person's son or daughter; a grandson or a granddaughter

grandparent (GRAND-pair-unt): the father or mother of a person's father or mother; a grandfather or a grandmother

hamburger (HAM BERG-er): ground meat from a cow; such meat cooked and put between two pieces of bread

hepatitis B (HEP-a-TIGHT-us B): an STD that can cause death.

HIV (H-I-V): an STD that often leads to AIDS and death

HSV (H-S-V) another name for genital herpes

information (IN-for-MAY-shun): facts, news

jealous (JEL-us): not liking another person because he has something you wish you had

magazine (MAG-a-ZEEN): a publication printed at set times usually with a paper cover and stories and pictures by different people

mature (Muh-toor): full age, fully developed as a person

media (MEE-dee-a): such things as newspapers, radio and televison considered together

mental (MENT-l): having to do with the mind

papillomavirus (PAP-a-LO-ma-VI-rus): the most common STD

penicillin (PEN-a-SIL-un): a medicine used to treat some STDs

physical (FIZ-ee-cul): having to do with things we can see and feel; a person's body

PID (P-I-D) — an STD that often leaves women unable to have children

provision (pro-VIZH-un): providing for or preparing for something

relationship (re-LA-shun-SHIP): connected together in some way such as family or work

reproductive organs (RE-pro-DUCK-tive OR-guns): the parts of the body that make it possible for people to have children

respected (re-SPECT-ud): to feel or show honor toward another person

secure (see-CURE): safe; free from fear or care

society (so-SI-a-t): all the people in an area or country

STD (S-T-D)— sexually transmitted disease; a disease that is usually passed from one person to another through having sex

syphilis (SIF-a-lus): a common STD that is easily passed from one person to another; it can lead to the break down of the body in many ways

television (TEL-a-VIZH-un): a kind of radio with pictures

tobacco (toe-BACK-o): a plant used mostly for smoking

trichomoniasis (TRIK-o-mo-NI-a-sis): an STD that effects women more than men and may cause cancer

virgin (VER-jun): a person, especially a woman, who has never had sex

wart: a small, usually hard growth on the skin

wine cooler: wine made weaker by adding something like the liquid of a fruit such as an apple

Endnotes

Chapter 1: Why Does True Love Wait?

1. Jacqueline F. de Gaston, Larry Jensen, and Stan Weed, "A Closer Look at Adolescent Sexual Activity," *Journal of Youth and Adolescence* 24, no. 4 (1995): 469-74.
2. Melissa Healy, "Clinton Frees $250 Million for Sex Abstinence Teaching," *Los Angeles Times*, 1 March 1997, sec. A, p. 12.
3. S.L. Hofferth, J.R. Kahn, and W. Baldwin, "Premarital Sexual Activity among U.S. Teenager Women over the Past Three Decades," *Family Planning Perspective* 19 (1987): 45-53.
4. Jerry Abejo, "Citing Drop in Teen Pregnancy, Report Credits Range of Factors," *The Philadelphia Inquirer*, 25 April 2001; <inq.philly.com>.
5. Centers for Disease Control News Release, "Teen Sex Down New Study Shows," May 1997; <www.cdc.gov/od/oc/media/pressrel/teensex.htm>.
6. Ibid.
7. National Center for Health Statistics Press Release, "Teen Sex Down New Study Shows," May 1, 1997; <www.hhs.gov/news/press/1997pres/970501.html>.
8. "The Naked Truth," *Newsweek* (May 8, 2000): 58.
9. Laurie Goodstein and Marjorie Connelly, "Teen-Age Poll Finds Support for Tradition," *New York Times*, 30 April 1998.
10. Kaiser Family Foundation and *YM* magazine, "National Survey of Teens: Teens Talk about Dating, Intimacy, and Their Sexual Experiences," *YM* magazine (May 1998): 5.
11. International Communications Research, "The Cautious Generation? Teens Tell Us about Sex, Virginity, and 'The Talk'" (a summary of findings from two nationally representative surveys of teenagers conducted by the National Campaign to Prevent Teen Pregnancy, International Communications Research, April 27, 2000), 5.
12. P. Beauman and H. Bruckner, "Power in Numbers: Peer Effects on Adolescent Girls' Sexual Debut and Pregnancy" (Washington, D.C.: The National Campaign to Prevent Teen Pregnancy, 1999).

Chapter 2: Young People and Sex Before Marriage

1. Kaiser Family Foundation, *Sexually Transmitted Diseases in America: How Many Cases and at What Cost?* (Menlo Park, Calif.: Kaiser Family Foundation, 1998); <www.kff.org/content/archive/1445/std_rel.pdf>.
2. The Institute of Medicine, *The Hidden Epidemic--Confronting Sexually Transmitted Disease*, ed. Thomas R. Eng and William T. Butler (Washington, D.C.: National Academy Press, 1997): 33.
3. The Medical Institute, "National Guidelines for Sexuality and Character Education" (Austin, Tex.: The Medical Institute, 1996): 5.
4. The Institute of Medicine, *Hidden Epidemic*, 39.
5. Joe S. McIlhaney Jr., M.D., *Sex: What You Don't Know Can Kill You* (Grand Rapids: Baker, 1997), 20.
6. D. Rusk et al., "Analysis of Invasive Squamous Cell Carcinoma of the Vulva and Vulvar Intraepithelial Neoplasia for the Presence of Human Papilloma Virus DNA," *American Journal of Obstetrics and Gynecology* 77 (1991): 918.
7. House Committee on Commerce, Ronald O. Valdiserri, M.D. speaking to the Subcommittee on Health and Environment on cervical cancer, *Congressional Record* (16 March 1999), 18-22.
8. The Institute of Medicine, *Hidden Epidemic*, 10.
9. T.S. Quinn, Review of *The Hidden Epidemic: Confronting Sexually Transmitted Diseases*, The Institute of Medicine, ed. Thomas R. Eng and William T. Butler, 1997, *New England Journal of Medicine* 337, no 16 (October 16, 1997): 1177-78.
10. Thomas E. Elkins, M.D., "Infectious Aspects of Contraceptive Practices" (paper, University of Michigan Medical Center, 1992), 10.
11. The Institute of Medicine, *Hidden Epidemic*, 10.
12. The Medical Institute, "Sexuality and Character Education," 5.
13. McIlhaney, *What You Don't Know*, 79.
14. Maggie Gallagher, "Elegy for Father's Day," *Investment Business Daily*, 14 June 1996, p. 6.
15. R.A. Maynard, ed., *Kids Having Kids: A Robin Hood Foundation Special Report on the Costs of Adolescent Childbearing* (New York: Robin Hood Foundation. 1996): 1-2.
16. Joshua Mann, M.D., Joe S. McIlhaney Jr., M.D., and Curtis C. Stine, M.D., *Building Healthy Futures: Tools for Helping Adolescents Avoid or Delay the Onset of Sexual Activity*. (Austin, Tex.: The Medical Institute, 2000): 19.

Chapter 3: The High Cost of Sex before Marriage

1. Joshua Mann, M.D., Joe S. McIlhaney Jr., M.D., and Curtis C. Stone, M.D., *Building Healthy Futures: Tools for Helping Adolescents Avoid or Delay the Onset of Sexual Activity* (Austin, Tex.: The Medical Institute, 2000): 4.
2. The Medical Institute, "Abstinence and 'Safer Sex' Sexuality Education: A Comparison" (Austin, Tex.: The Medical Institute, 1999): 20.

3. Lynn Smith, "What's the Matter with Kids Today? Their Parents," *Los Angeles Times*, 19 May 1996, sec. E, p. 3.
4. Diane Duston, "Sons of Teen Moms 3 Times More Likely to Wind Up in Jail," *South Coast Today*, 13 June 1996; <www.s-t.com/daily/06-96/06-14-96/a02wn018.htm>.
5. R.A. Maynard, ed., *Kids Having Kids: A Robin Hood Foundation Special Report on the Costs of Adolescent Childbearing* (New York: Robin Hood Foundation, 1996), 7-11.
6. Duston, "Sons of Teen Moms."
7. Maynard, *Kids Having Kids*, 7-ll, 14.
8. Susan Richardson, "An Overlooked Weapon in the Battle of Teen Pregnancy: Self-Esteem," *Austin American-Statesman*, 5 March 1998.

Chapter 4: Children in Grown-up Bodies
1. Suzanne Fields, "Condom nation," *The Washington Times: National Weekly Edition*, 27 April 1997.
2. Josh McDowell, *Why Wait: What You Need to Know about the Teen Sexuality Crisis* (Nashville, Tenn.: Thomas Nelson, 1987), 79.
3. Kaiser Family Foundation and *YM* magazine, "National Survey of Teens: Teens Talk about Dating, Intimacy, and Their Sexual Experiences," *YM* magazine (May 1998): 5
4. Andrea E. Bonny, M.D. and Frank M. Biro, M.D., "Recognizing and Treating STDs in Adolescent Girls," *Contemporary Pediatrics* (March 1998): 139.
5. Anne Pandolf, "Teen Sex from Drug Use: Odds Are Greater If Teenagers Use Alcohol, Drugs," *ABC News*, December 7, 1999; <abcnews.go.com/sections/living/Daily News/teensex991207.html>.
6. J. Thomas Fitch, M.D., "How Effective Are Condoms in Preventing Pregnancy and STDs in Adolescents?" (Austin, Tex.: The Medical Institute, July 1997): 2-4.
7. Tom Luster and Stephen A. Small, "Sexual Abuse History and Number of Sex Partners among Female Adolescents," *Family Planning Perspectives* 29 (1997): 204-11.

Chapter 5: Growing Up in a World Where Wrong Is Right
1. Anita Manning, "Teen Girls No Longer Enjoy an Age of Innocence," *USA Today*, 6 October 1997, sec. D, p. 4.
2. Haddon Robinson, ed., "CT Classic: Sex, Marriage and Divorce," *Christianity Today* (December 14, 1992).

Chapter 6: The Media's Influence
1. Alice Fryling, "Why Wait for Sex?" *InterVarsity Christian Fellowship of the USA Student Leadership Journal* (spring 1995): 1.
2. Abbylin Sellers, *The Sexual Abstinence Message Causes Positive Changes in Adolescent Behavior: A Circumstantial Review of Relevant Studies* (Santa Barbara, Calif.: Westmont College, 1998), 1-3.
3. G. Gerbner, *Women and Minorities: A Study in Casting and Fate* (a report to the Screen Actors Guild and the American Federation of Radio and Television Artists, June 1993), 3.
4. M. Morgan, "Television and School Performance," in *Adolescent Medicine: Adolescents and the Media* (Philadelphia: Hanley & Belfus, 1993). 607-22.
5. J.D. Klein et al., "Adolescents' Risky Behavior and Mass Media Use," *Pediatrics* 92, no. 1 (1993):24-31.
6. Bradley S. Greenberg et al., "Sex Content on Soaps and Prime-Time Television Series Most Viewed by Adolescents," in *Media, Sex and the Adolescent*, ed. Bradley S. Greenberg, Jane D. Brown, and Nancy L. Buerkel-Rothfuss (Cresskill, N.J.: Hampton, 1993), 29-44.
7. Bradley S. Greenberg and R. Linsangan, "Gender Differences in Adolescents' Media Use, Exposure to Sexual Content and Parental Mediation," in *Media, Sex and the Adolescent*, ed. Greenberg, Brown, and Buerkel-Rothfuss, 134-44.
8. A. Soderman, Bradley S. Greenberg, and R. Linsangan, "Pregnant and Non-Pregnant Adolescents' Television and Movie Experiences," in *Media, Sex and the Adolescent*, ed. Greenberg, Brown, and Buerkel-Rothfuss, 163-73.
9. Kaiser Family Foundation, "Sex on TV," a biennial report (Menlo Park, Calif.: Kaiser Family Foundation, January 2001): 2.
10. Gene Edward Veith, "Crass Wasteland," *World* (March 3, 2001): 14.
11. N.L. Buerkel-Rothfuss and J.S. Strouse, "Media Exposure and Perceptions of Sexual Behaviors: the Cultivation Hypothesis Moves to the Bedroom," in *Media, Sex and the Adolescent*, ed. Greenberg, Brown, and Buerkel-Rothfuss, 225-47.
12. Bradley S. Greenberg and R.W. Busselle, *Soap Operas and Sexual Activity* (a report prepared for the Kaiser Family Foundation and presented at the Soap Summit, October 21, 1994).
13. Veith, "Crass Wasteland," 14.

Chapter 7: A "Love Hunger" at Home
1. Laurence Steinberg, "Failure Outside the Classroom," *The Wall Street Journal*, 11 July 1996, p. 10.
2. R.W. Blum and P.M. Rinehart, *Reducing the Risk: Connections That Make a Difference in the Lives of Youth* (Minneapolis, Minn.: University of Minnesota Division of General Pediatrics and Adolescent Health, 1997), 15, 17, 19.
3. Ann Landers, "Sorry, Ladies: Cuddling Second in Sex Survey," *Los Angeles Times*, 25 November 1995.
4. Lisa Collier Cool, "The Dreaded Talk," *Ladies Home Journal* (March 2001).

5. YMCA of the USA, "Talking with Teens: The YMCA Teen and Parent Survey Final Report," *The YMCA-2000 Strong Family Survey* (New York, Global Strategy Group, 2000): 5.
6. Ibid., 1.

Chapter 8: Young People in Need Turn to Sex
1. Nancy Gibbs, "How Should We Teach Our Children about Sex?" *Time* (May 24, 1993): 63.
2. "The 1994 Churched Youth Survey" (Dallas: Josh McDowell Ministry, 1994): 62.
3. Kaiser Family Foundation and *YM* magazine, "National Survey of Teens: Teens Talk about Dating, Intimacy, and Their Sexual Experiences," *YM* magazine (May 1998): 5.
4. Liana R. Clark, M.D., "Teen Sex Blues," *The Journal of the American Medical Association* 273, no. 24 (June 18, 1995): 1969-70.

Chapter 9: Everyone Is Doing It, So Why Should We Wait?
1. Ann Landers, "Study Finds Girls Regret Having Sex," *Austin American-Statesman*, 20 October 1996, sec. E, p. 2.
2. Jacqueline F. de Gaston, Larry Jensen, and Stan Weed, "A Closer Look at Adolescent Sexual Activity," *Journal of Youth and Adolescence* 24, no. 4 (1995): 465.

Chapter 11: The Physical Reasons to Wait
1. Heather Farish, "Better U.S. Teens Abstain Than Opt for European Way," *Houston Chronicle*, 16 February 1999.
2. Agneta Andersson-Ellstrom, Lars Forssman, and Ian Milsom, "The Relationship between Knowledge about Sexually Transmitted Diseases and Actual Sexual Behavior in a Group of Teenage Girls," *Genitourinary Medicine* 72 (1996): 32-36.
3. Joe S. McIlhaney Jr., M.D., *Sex: What You Don't Know Can Kill You* (Grand Rapids: Baker, 1997), 22.
4. Lawrence K. Altman, "3 Million HIV Infections Added Worldwide in '96," *Denver Post*, 28 November 1996, sec. A, p. 24.
5. "Around the U. S.," *Dallas Morning News*, 2 December 1994, sec. A, p. 10.
6. *Seventeen* (May 1990): 149-51.
7. Robin DeRosa, "HIV Study," *USA Today*, 9 February 1998, sec. B, p. 8.
8. "Arm Yourself against AIDS," MSNBC, June 29, 2000; <http://msnbc.com/modules/quizzes/loadquiz.htm>.
9. "HIV Prevention Act of 1997," *Washington Watch Policy Update*.
10. Office of National AIDS Policy, "Youth and HIV/AIDS: An American Agenda," March 1996; <www.niaid.nih.gov/publications/dateline/full/0996.htm>.
11. Sexuality Information and Education Council of the U.S., "Fact Sheet: Sexually Transmitted Diseases in the United States," *Siecus Report* 25, no. 3 (1997).
12. The Medical Institute, "Chlamydia Trachomatis: The Most Common Bacterial Sexually Transmitted Disease in the United States," *Sexual Health Update Newsletter* 3, no. 3 (fall 1995).
13. Andrea E. Bonney, M.D., and Frank M. Biro, M.D., "Recognizing and Treating STDs in Adolescent Girls," *Contemporary Pediatrics* (March 1998): 126.
14. L. Westrom, "Incidence, Prevalence, and Trends of Acute Pelvic Inflammatory Disease and Its Consequences in Industrialized Countries," *American Journal of Obstetrics and Gynecology* 138: 880-92.
15. A.E. Washington and P. Katz, "Cost of and Payment Source for Pelvic Inflammatory Disease," *Journal of the American Medical Association* 266, no 18 (1991): 2565-9.
16. Ibid.
17. Sexuality Information and Education Council, "Fact Sheet."
18. Ibid.
19. Bonny and Biro, "Recognizing and Treating STDs," 119, 123, 131.
20. John R. Diggs Jr., M.D., *Gonorrhea* (Sioux Falls, S. Dak.: Abstinence Clearing House, 2000), 1.
21. W.E. Lafferty et al., "Herpes Simplex Virus Type I as a Cause of Genital Herpes: Impact on Surveillance and Prevention," *Journal of Infectious Diseases* 181 (April 2000):1454-57.
22. John R. Diggs Jr., M.D. *Herpes Simplex* (Sioux Falls, S. Dak.: Abstinence Clearinghouse, 2000), 1.
23. Division of Health, Wisconsin Department of Health and Social Services, "Women and VD," 1994.
24. National Institutes of Health Consensus Development Program, "Cervical Cancer," *Consensus Development Statements* 14, no. 1 (April 1-3, 1996): <odp.od.nih.gov/consensus/cons/102/102_intro.htm>.
25. R. Whitley et al., "A Controlled Trial Comparing Vidarabine with Acyclovir in Neonatal Herpes Simplex Virus Infection: Infectious Diseases Collaborative Antiviral Study Group," *New England Journal of Medicine* 324 (1991): 444-49.
26. National Institutes of Health, "Cervical Cancer."
27. Abstinence Clearinghouse, *Abstinence Clearinghouse Fact Sheet on Human Papilloma Virus.*
28. William Archer III, M.D., *Sexual Health Update Newsletter* 7, no. 3 (fall 1999).
29. House, Ronald O. Valdiserri, M.D., speaking for the Committee on Commerce to the Subcommittee on Health and Environment on Cervical Cancer (16 March 1999), 3-5.
30. John Diggs, "A Perspective on the Medical Implications of Virginity Pledge among Teens," *The Physicians Consortium* (January 5, 2001).
31. Centers for Disease Control, "Ten Leading Nationally Notifiable Diseases--U.S., 1995," *Morbidity and Mortality Weekly Report* 45 (1996): 883-84.

32. House, Valdiserri, 24.

33. V.P. Smetnik and L.G. Tumilovitch, *Non-Surgical Gynecology* (St. Petersburg: Sotis Publishing, 1995).

34. McIlhaney, *What You Don't Know*, 54-55.

35. Ibid.

36. Smetnik and Tumilovitch, *Non-Surgical Gynecology*.

37. J.M. Walboomers et al., "Human Papillomavirus Is a Necessary Cause of Invasive Cervical Cancer Worldwide," *Journal of Pathology* 189 (1999): 12-19, quoted in *Sexual Health Update Newsletter* 8, no. 1 (spring 2000): 1-2.

Chapter 13: Reasons to Wait Because of Relationships

1. Karen S. Peterson, "At 20, a Soul Mate is a Cool Concept," *USA Today*, 13 June 2001, sec. A, p. 1.

2. Elizabeth Thomson and Ugo Colella, "Cohabitation and Marital Stability: Quality or Commitment?" *Journal of Marriage and the Family* 54 (1992): 259-67.

3. Joshua Mann, M.D., Joe S. McIlhaney Jr., M.D. and Curtis C. Stine, M.D., *Building Healthy Futures: Tools for Helping Adolescents Avoid or Delay the Onset of Sexual Activity* (Austin, Tex.: The Medical Institute, 2000), 18-19.

Chapter 14: The Spiritual Reasons to Wait

1. Originally published in Josh McDowell, *Givers, Takers, and Other Kinds of Lovers* (Wheaton, Ill.: Tyndale, 1981): 19-21.

Chapter 15: Why "Safe Sex" Is Not Safe

1. Amy Stephens, "The Kaiser Report: Truth or Dare?" October 23, 2000: <www.family.org/cforum/editorials/a0015083.html>.

2. Joe S. McIlhaney Jr., M.D., *Sex: What You Don't Know Can Kill You* (Grand Rapids: Baker, 1997), 63-64.

3. John R. Diggs Jr., M.D., letter to author, 26 January 2001.

4. Alan Mozes, "Do Condoms and Seat Belts Promote Risk Taking?" Excite News, January 28, 2000; <news.excite.com/news/r/000128/18/health-psc>.

5. John D. Hartigan, "The Disastrous Results of Condom Distribution Programs," *Family Research Council* (March 29, 2001).

6. Heather Farish, "The Whole Story on Sex," Family Research Council: Press Room, March 29, 2001.

7. Joshua Mann, M D., Joe S. McIlhaney Jr., M.D., and Curtis S. Stine, M.D., *Building Healthy Futures: Tools for Helping Adolescents Avoid or Delay the Onset of Sexual Activity* (Austin, Tex.: The Medical Institute, 2000), 17.

8. Editorial, "Short Takes: Advertising Abstinence," *The Atlanta Journal and Constitution*, 22 February 1997, sec. A, p. 12.

9. SIECUS and Roper Starch Organization, "Teens Talk about Sex: Adolescent Sexuality in the '90s" (SIECUS and Roper Starch Organization, April 11, 1995): 25.

10. Dale Stone, letter to author.

Chapter 16: Develop a Caring Relationship with Your Children

1. Melissa Grace, "Teen Pregnancies Raising Crime Costs," *Santa Barbara (Calif.) News-Press,* 22 June 1996.

2. Ibid.

3. This section is adapted from Josh McDowell, *How To Help Your Child Say No to Sexual Pressure* (Waco, Tex.: Word, 1987), 45-54.

Chapter 17: Urge a Close Relationship with Christ

1. Previously published in Josh McDowell, *Why Wait: What You Need to Know about the Teen Sexuality Crisis* (Nashville, Tenn.: Thomas Nelson, 1987), 404-09.

Chapter 18: Teach Sexual Values at Home

1. Donna Rice Hughes, "For Parents Only," Kids Online, 2000; <www.protectkids.com/fc/4parentsonly.htm>.

Chapter 19: Help Children Develop the Strength to Say No

1. R.W. Blum and P.M. Rinehart, *Reducing the Risk: Connections that Make a Difference in the Lives of Youth* (Minneapolis, Minn.: University of Minnesota Division of General Pediatrics and Adolescent Health, 1997), 30.

Chapter 20: Help Young People Set Limits for Dating

1. Adapted from Josh McDowell, *How to Help Your Child Say No to Sexual Pressure* (Waco, Tex.: Word, 1987), 112-23.

2. Kaiser Family Foundation and *YM* magazine, "National Survey of Teens: Teens Talk about Dating, Intimacy, and Their Sexual Experiences," *YM* magazine (May 1998): 5.